Brim Full of Passion

Wasim Khan — from the ghetto to pro cricket and beyond

Wasim Khan with Alan Wilkinson

Brim Full of Passion

Wasim Khan — from the ghetto to pro cricket and beyond

Foreword by Wasim Akram

Chance to shine
BRINGING CRICKET TO STATE SCHOOLS

PIP
POLLINGER IN PRINT

Pollinger Limited
9 Staple Inn
Holborn
LONDON
WC1V 7QH

www.pollingerltd.com

First published by EPB Publishers Pte Ltd 2006
This large print edition published by Pollinger in Print 2007

Copyright © Wasim Khan 2006
All rights reserved

The moral right of the author has been asserted

A CIP catalogue record is available from the British Library

ISBN 978-1-905665-24-2

No part of this book may be reproduced, stored in a retrieval system, or transmitted in any form, or by any means, electronic, mechanical or otherwise, without prior written permission from Pollinger Limited

Contents

Acknowledgements		6
Foreword		7
Chapter 1	The bat	9
Chapter 2	The balls	19
Chapter 3	Passage to Edgbaston	26
Chapter 4	The talent scout	42
Chapter 5	Handling cutlery, and other useful skills	54
Chapter 6	How many cricketers can you get in a Mini?	59
Chapter 7	Losing Dad	68
Chapter 8	Give Wasim the menu, he knows about this stuff	82
Chapter 9	At last – a contract	93
Chapter 10	Bright lights of Sydney	102
Chapter 11	Living a double life	108
Chapter 12	'I think you're playing'	133
Chapter 13	Double winner	155
Chapter 14	Swings and roundabouts	176
Chapter 15	'Thought you dark fellers could run!'	194
Chapter 16	Warwickshire: the end of an era	213
Chapter 17	A new start at Hove	234
Chapter 18	Grizzly times on the south coast	251
Chapter 19	12th man with a twist	281
Chapter 20	Opening bat for hire – cheap	302
Chapter 21	Thanks for the memories	319
Chapter 22	Back where I started	329
Chapter 23	The ghetto boy and the Governor	340

Dedication

For mum, Raheena, my wife Salma and everyone who has been there for me.

Foreword

I AM delighted to provide a foreword for Wasim's book.

In life there are many who use their experiences in a positive way to make a difference to the lives of people through their strength, dedication and commitment.

Wasim is one of those people. Through playing professional cricket he has learnt valuable lessons, which have now enabled him to be at the forefront of one of the biggest grass-roots initiatives ever undertaken in sport.

As a cricketer, having played against him, I thought that he had a big heart. He scored a few against me, but as a person he lives his life with integrity and passion, encompassing the family values he has so strongly instilled in him.

I remember playing against my namesake at Old Trafford in 1995 and being impressed by what I saw. It's a shame he never really cracked it and went on to play at a higher level. With anything in life luck and destiny play a big part, and I believe that sometimes your real purpose and contentment in life comes in a different way than you first imagined. I was fortunate to play many years of Test cricket and be successful at that higher level, playing against the best and achieving a great deal individually and for my country, Pakistan. Wasim is now at his highest level, being part of something where his passion will shine through.

His book deals with the issues raised by growing up within a Pakistani family environment in England, and ultimately deals with the highs and lows we all experience in life.

Wasim Akram
Former Lancashire and Pakistan cricketer

CHAPTER 1

The bat

THE BLADE of the bat feels like silk as I run my gloved hand up and down, up and down, trying to concentrate, trying to forget, trying to blot out the past.

It's not easy. Even as the new bowler marks out his run, scuffing up the dust from the scorched earth, wiping the sweat off the ball with a cloth, my mind is in danger of wandering. There are a lot of memories pressing in right now.

Seven years on the ground staff; four years playing Magoo cricket for the seconds; then the whole of last season, knocking off hundred after hundred around the out-grounds as the first team romped to that historic treble without any help from me: Championship, one-day Cup and Sunday League; and then, finally, the injury to Nick Knight, the call-up, and a decent little run of scores until the England man recovers and I'm shoved aside once more.

Back to the seconds. Another four hundreds. What more can they want, in the name of God? What do I have to do to get into the team? And then, at last – another chance.

There can't be many more, can there? August already, Friday 11 August – as if I'll ever forget that date.

But at the crease there, with the sun blazing down – and the hot breath of Middlesex on our necks at the top of the Championship – I *have* to forget. Everything. And concentrate. It's a team game, isn't it?

I twirl the bat and caress the blade one more time, trying to put out of my mind the fear that's crept in there over all the years of waiting and hoping and explaining to friends and neighbours that I *hadn't* failed, that I was a top reserve in a great county side. Dermot Reeve, Gladstone Small, Brian Lara, Nick Knight. I was competing with the best in the country. Maybe it was true what some people were saying – that I'd walk into most county sides. I wanted to believe it, sure I did. But the mighty Warwickshire? No, not just yet...

All they knew about back in Small Heath was headlines, hat-tricks and hundreds. That Wasim, he can't be that good, otherwise he'd be a first-team fixture. Other voices crowded into my head. Face the facts, man: how many Asians have ever made it at county level? Your face'll never fit. You should've concentrated on education, like your parents told you. Look at your old mate Asraf – a lawyer already with a big car and a hot young wife.

CHAPTER 1 : THE BAT

But here I was, back in the First XI for the trip to Southampton, my captain Dermot Reeve at the other end, inching my way towards a maiden first-class hundred. I wondered how many of the old gang would be watching on Teletext, like they had when I made my debut.

I was starting to hear the commentator in my head, the commentator who'd been there since I was a kid listening in the dead of night to Test matches from Down Under. 'And now a slightly nervous Wasim – 93 not out – taps his bat in the crease, as Udal turns to walk back to his mark.'

Come on, Shaun. You know it's going to happen. You know my luck's in today. Dropped twice on 85? What more proof do you want? Let's just get it over with.

And here it comes, right on leg stump, just where I want it, perfect length. 'And Wasim clips it away for four...' to a ripple of polite applause from a sparse crowd, half stupefied by the sun and the beer and the drowsiness that settles over a county ground after lunch. They haven't the faintest idea what this means to me.

Dermot motions to me to stay cool. I stroke the bat once more, those memories already heading for the exits of my mind as the inevitable moment approaches. You can't argue with Fate. Not when your luck's in.

And then, as Udal fiddles with his boot and needlessly consults with his captain over some minor field change – desperately looking around for anything that'll disrupt my flow, I allow myself one more touch of my bat... and here we go: another memory's elbowed its way to the front of my mind.

*****

I'm in the shed with the gang and we're trying everything we can think of to put a finish to the new bat. The shape's as good as you could hope for, right down to the slope of the shoulders. But it's all splintered at the edges, rough to the touch. It'll rip the balls to shreds, no matter that we wrap them with that electrical tape we nicked from Malik's store. And then someone – probably Parvaz – brings in a piece of broken glass with a nice clean edge to it. Sharp as a razor. Must have been from one of those milk bottles we chucked out when we grabbed the crate off Mrs Ahmed's doorstep for a wicket and they shattered on the pavement and we all took off like the wind.

We start scraping, and by the end of the afternoon we've got something that not only looks but feels like the real thing. Silky, with that special sheen a cricket bat ought to have.

CHAPTER 1 : THE BAT

The wood was never going to be a problem. I just waited till Dad was at work at the bakery and Mum was busy cooking up my favourite curry, and sneaked down the end of the garden there in Somerville Road. The fence was decrepit enough when we moved in. They all were. Good enough for a bunch of Asians in an inner city. With all the gaps that had been knocked in them over the years we could just nip through as we careered from one garden to the next in pursuit of lost balls – or hurried home with scrumped apples stuffed up our shirts. I leaned back, gave the fence a mighty wallop with my right foot – and out came the plank like a rotten tooth.

So far so good, but how to carve it into shape? It had to be right. When we were young, sure, we'd play with anything, even a bit of busted clothes-prop; but we were older now – 10, 11 – and we'd already seen that boy from Hugh Road who ponced about with his proper bat, red rubber handle and all, as if he was some bloody Maharajah. We had to do something: we had our pride, our reputation to think about, the street's reputation. We couldn't go on with bits of scrap timber – although it wasn't so bad now that we had that pair of old gardening gloves we'd got off Paul's Dad to protect us against the splinters.

'We need a knife,' said Azeem, after gouging a few lumps out of the plank with an old screwdriver he'd got from his Dad's shed. 'This is no good.'

We looked at each other. 'So who's got a knife?'

'You're kidding. My Dad caught Nadeem with one and all hell broke loose. Made him throw it in the canal!' We never said a word. Iftikhar's Dad had been in the Army, and we knew we couldn't mess with him.

In the end there was nothing for it. 'We've got knives,' I said. 'Three of them.' Paul laughed. 'Always trying to be one up on everybody else, eh Waz?' Paul was English. Well, Irish. They all looked the same to us. The first time he came to our house and saw us all sat scooping up curry with our chapattis and fingers he just stood there with his mouth open. He soon realised, as the street filled up with Asians, that he was destined to be the first white Pakistani. And sure enough he was: a few years later they were the last white family remaining on the street, until the unfortunate death of his parents.

So it was down to me to get the knife – with Paul's help. The kitchen drawer was a rickety old affair, and Mum had the cupboard door tied to it with string, otherwise the whole thing could collapse any time.

CHAPTER 1 : THE BAT

'She's tied it with a knot, man.'
'So?' Paul looked perplexed. 'Just untie it.'
'Then what?'
'Tie it back up again, man.'
I had to explain to Paul that I still couldn't tie a shoelace properly.

So there I was, wrapping the gleaming blade in a floor-cloth and sliding it carefully down my trousers while Paul rearranged the string the way Mum had left it.

'This knife, it never keeps an edge,' Mum complained in Punjabi as she stood at the kitchen table slicing onions next day. Is cannot understand it. All that time saving up for it, as well. It's a mystery to me.' Dad put down his Daily Jang, took the knife and sharpened it for her on the back step, but next day it was the same again. 'Blunt as anything. We should take it back and complain,' Mum muttered to herself as I slipped silently out the door to join the gang and resume a four-day Test Match against Hugh Road.

*****

'Come on, Shaun, look at him.' The lads in the field are trying to wind me up, but it's too late for that. I'm on my way, in the zone, twirling my bat, itching to get after him.

'Put him out of his misery. He's never been here before.'

You can always count on your fellow professionals to make your maiden hundred a memorable affair. Udal grins, wipes his sweaty hand on his trousers, grips the ball – fingers spread across the seam – and trots up to the wicket. One thing I can be sure of: he's not going to wander down leg-side this time. He doesn't. He drags it just outside off, slightly short, and I give it the full treatment. With a single puff of dust it's off, like a missile, across a lightning fast outfield.

'And there's his hundred!' I never saw it hit the boundary boards. My eyes were raised to the heavens, half blinded by the sun – and, I might as well admit it, a tear or two. Next moment Dermot was at my side. A single word of congratulation, and then it's 'Fucking concentrate, you hear me? We've got a game to win, so dig in.'

Dig in? After what I've been through? For the first time in an age I played with absolute abandon. The bowlers were wilting, but I was suddenly finding new reserves of energy. For a glorious hour or so that afternoon everything I tried came off. Cuts, pulls, glances, lofted drives. I was soon hooking one over deep square to bring up the 150, and 20 minutes later I was sitting under a cold shower as tea was taken with me on 160 not out, wondering whether

CHAPTER 1 : THE BAT

this time, maybe, I'd done enough to be taken seriously. What did it need? A double ton? Well, if that's what they wanted...

But it wasn't to be. I'd been batting for seven hours now, and what with the heat and the emotion I was finally starting to weaken. As the prospect of the magic 200 crept into my weary mind, I took a swipe at Cardigan Connor's slower ball... and was bowled for 181. For a moment I was angry with myself. You always feel disappointed to be out, no matter how many runs you've got on the board. Later I found out I'd made the record books: the highest score ever by a Warwickshire player at Southampton. That helped.

As I walked back to the pavilion my teammates and the spectators gave me a standing ovation; in the dressing room Ashley Giles gave me a hug and a high five; Keith Piper, who'd got himself out for 99 as I smashed the ball around the ground, was waiting for me with a cold can of Coke. Back in my hotel room that night there were messages on the TV screen from players who'd helped me along the way like Andy Lloyd and K.D. Smith, from my family, from my friends back in Small Heath. And there was news that Parvaz – the kid I'd played with in the street, with the milk crates and the taped-up ball – had got his first five-wicket haul for neighbouring Worcestershire. There was a call too from Pete Bolland, who'd singled me out in the school playground all those years ago. Then, just before bed, a call from my sister Raheena, who'd sat all evening glued to the telly and recorded every last clip off the *Central News* bulletins. I fell asleep with a big stupid grin on my face.

CHAPTER 2

The balls

CARVING the bat had been a labour of love. When you take a six-inch plank and try to whittle the upper half down to the size of a normal bat-handle – trust me, you've got a job on. But what I lacked in material wealth I made up for in patience. I put in an hour or so every day, and gradually it took shape. Sometimes my mates would help, but they soon got bored. Eventually, after four long weeks, I'd got something that looked like a bat. And straight away the arguments began. What were we to put on it? All the bats we saw on the telly had something on them – a bit of writing, or a design of some sort.

Gary, the Jamaican boy next door, knew straight away what to do. Put BUZZ on it in big letters. 'Why not?' he said. 'You done most of da work, man.'

Tariq agreed. 'Yeah, the maker's name. Like on the telly. You're the maker. Stick your name on it.'

They started calling me Buzz when that British Telecom advert first appeared, back in the seventies. I was such a scrawny little kid they took one look at Buzzby, the ragged crow perched on the telephone lines, and the name just seemed to fit. Even my family used it sometimes.

'You kidding?' I said. 'What if my Mum saw it, or my Dad?'

'What if they did?'

'And then they ask me where I got it? Don't be stupid.' I took the bat home every night, sure – even kept it next to my bed; but I never let on that I'd made it. I didn't want them asking awkward questions. As far as they were concerned it was just some old bat that belonged to the gang.

In the end we decided on W.C.C.C. – Warwickshire County Cricket Club. It was Paul Kenna's idea. He said they were our local team, like the Blues, but in cricket. Birmingham City we understood – after all, we lived in Birmingham, didn't we? Supported the Blues. Watched the crowds walking down there on a winter's Saturday and tried to work out how to get in for nothing. Copied songs we'd heard taking the piss out of Villa. Yeah, we knew about Birmingham okay. But where was this Warwickshire? Well, who cared? Certainly not me, as I borrowed Mum's knife again and carved the initials onto the face of the bat.

Later, other kids around the neighbourhood started to make their own bats. More

CHAPTER 2 : THE BALLS

and more appeared, some of them a bit shapeless, one or two quite good, but none of them as good as mine – and of course the garden fences took a right hammering. But who cared? Not us kids. We didn't need fences – we were in and out of each others' back yards regardless.

It was a real multicultural street we grew up in: West Indians, Pakistanis, Indians, Bengalis, Irish, English... but we kids were more or less colour-blind. Sure, we could see the differences, especially when Gary's Mum launched into us in her Jamaican dialect after we'd nicked her clothes-prop to get a ball off the roof. We nodded in agreement with her, muttered an apology and scuttled away without understanding a word she'd said. When you're a kid, a ticking off is a ticking off in any language.

I carried my new bat with pride, never letting it out of my sight. No way was I going to lose it: it meant more to me than any possession I'd ever had. Balls were a different proposition. They don't grow on trees either, but as our batsmanship improved and our strength grew we were getting through two or three a week, hitting them further and further: onto roofs, where they nestled tantalisingly out of reach in someone's gutter, into our neighbours' gardens, once or twice through a window – and the street emptied faster than it did on Cup Final Day. Broken Pane Stopped Play. One day I hit a lofted drive my hero Ian Botham would've been proud of – and it landed in the back of a council lorry, disappeared down the street and round into Charles Road. We had a big fight over that – did we call it a six or could I keep on running till they got it back? Either way, it meant another expedition to the school play-ground.

Somerville Road School was good to us. It provided us with all the balls we could use – or should I say lose? Poor old Miss Francis. She took us for PE in the playground, and every lesson she issued yet another set of tennis-balls.

'Miss, Miss!'

'What is it, Wasim?'

'Miss, the ball went up on the roof, Miss!'

'Went up, Wasim? Of its own accord, I suppose?'

'Honest, Miss. It just went. The wind must've done it.'

'You'll really have to curb your enthusiasm, Wasim.'

'Yes, Miss. Sorry, Miss.'

And she'd produce another one – positively the last one I'd be allowed this week. Then after school we'd sneak back down the road, me, Nadeem, Paul and Gary,

CHAPTER 2 : THE BALLS

Azeem and Iftikhar, and squirm our way to the top of the gate, crawl ever so carefully over the spikes at the top, and then shin up the drain-pipe onto the flat roof of Classroom 8. By the end of the year we reckoned we'd collected 32 balls, and the caretaker was doing his nut.

'Miss Francis.'

'Yes, Mr Jones.'

'I've been up on the roof like you asked me to.'

'Oh good – did you get the balls?'

'There are no balls on that roof, Miss Francis.'

'But I saw Wasim hit two up there myself – yesterday morning.'

'Well, they ain't there now Miss Francis.'

'Miss, Miss!'

'Yes, Paul?'

'Maybe a vulture ate them, Miss.'

'There are no exotic birds in this part of Birmingham, Paul Kenna.'

'That's funny. My dad says all us kids are a lot of bloody vultures...'

Meanwhile our games became more sophisticated. We'd set up two milk crates in the middle of the street, and appoint members of the side to proper fielding positions – slips, gully, things we'd picked up off the telly or the radio commentaries. As early as the winter of 1979–80 I'd heard the broadcasts from Down Under, late at night or early mornings, as England fought for the Ashes. The jargon fascinated me, just as the game did. Eighteen months later came the amazing series in which England twice set the Aussies targets of under 150, and stuffed them both times – most famously at Headingley where, after Botham's amazing 149 not out in a follow-on innings, Bob Willis ate up his Weetabix and came steaming in to take 8 for 40-odd. Then, unbelievably, they repeated the treatment in the next game, Botham grabbing 5 for 11 in the second innings. These guys were now my heroes – and the fact that they were English never entered my mind. They were just sporting heroes. Super-men. I knew then that's what I wanted to be.

As I said, at this stage we kids in Somerville Road didn't really have what you'd call an ethnic consciousness. My mates knew that at my house we spoke Punjabi. I still do when I'm at home, or around older relatives. Guys like Paul and Gary, native English speakers, they were around my place often enough that they started speaking basic Punjabi. They'd come in and it'd be 'Assalam alakum, Mrs Khan' – hello, or God be with you – and Mum would be delighted. 'Thank you very much,

CHAPTER 2 : THE BALLS

Mrs Khan', they'd say. 'How are you today, Mrs Khan?' all in her native tongue. Mum thought they were so well-mannered and polite. Such nice boys. Why couldn't I be like that? Luckily she couldn't understand what we were saying among ourselves in English or she'd have been down on us like a ton of bricks. At the same time as Gary and the other white kids picked up basic Punjabi, we kids had learned most of our English off them – including all the swear-words we didn't want our parents to hear. It's what they call multiculturalism.

CHAPTER 3

Passage to Edgbaston

THE YEAR after the Botham-Willis series we heard some exciting news. More than exciting: breathtaking. Even Dad started talking about it. Pakistan were coming to England to play three Tests, and the first one was at Edgbaston, right at the beginning of our summer holidays.

'Where's Edgbaston?' Amjad, Parvaz and I were sitting in my neighbour's shed, which we broke into from time to time, on a cold, wet afternoon. Rain had stopped play. I mean serious rain – buckets of it, a tropical downpour – otherwise we would've been out there playing just the same as usual.

'Edgbaston? It's right here, man.'
'What, in Birmingham?'
'Yeah. Don't you know anything?'
'And Pakistan are playing England there?'
'That's what I said, didn't I?'
'Well, are we going then or what?'
Parvaz laughed. 'It costs a bloody fortune, man. And you have to wear a suit.'
'And a top hat,' Amjad said.
'And be a member.'

CHAPTER 3 : PASSAGE TO EDGBASTON

'What's that? Member of what? Member of Parliament?'

'Probably.'

'Bollocks to that,' I said. 'If Pakistan are playing we have to go. It's our homeland.'

Homeland. I'd heard Dad use the word, when he talked about sending half his wages there to keep his cousins and uncles going, or when a friend went back there to bury a relative or collect a bride, and it must have stirred something inside me. It stirred my mates all right. Okay, they said, we'll go.

Later that afternoon we listed the obstacles that stood in our way. There were only three.

'Our parents would never let us.'

'We don't know how to get to bloody Edgbaston.'

'We ain't got any money.'

Sometimes we had a bit of cash. I got a few pence pocket money every week – we all did – and in the footie season we'd stand in the streets around St Andrews and try to charge Blues fans for looking after their cars. But it was all 10 pences and coppers. Now we had to find enough to get us into a Test Match. Dream on.

But that's the point: kids do dream. They see what they want and they go for it, regardless. They don't have an adult's experience of failure and disappointment, so it never occurs to them that some things are out of reach. They just blunder their way forward, regardless of the consequences. Sometimes it's a good thing they have parents there to protect them from danger. Other times you look back and think, well, if any adult had known what we were planning they'd have stopped us there and then. And that would have been a pity. Anyway, it wasn't an issue in this event. We kept quiet. Didn't even tell our mates at first.

We thought up all sorts of wild ideas, but we never came up with one that would give us the money we needed. In the end we decided we'd just go down to Edgbaston and play it by ear. A bit like the England cricket team at that time, come to think of it. Maybe just being there would be excitement enough.

The match was due to start on Thursday 29 July. School broke up the previous Friday, so we had time to plan. We even had a dummy run, hopping the number 8 bus to Edgbaston and scouting around. All we learned was that the walls around the ground were high – too high to climb up, surely – and that it was a hell of a long walk back home.

The walls were a real problem. But maybe we could sling a rope over the top. It was Amjad's idea – and he was in the best

CHAPTER 3 : PASSAGE TO EDGBASTON

position to get hold of one. His Mum was a soft touch, not like Parvaz's or mine. They'd be all questions. What were we up to this time? Why would we need a rope? You're not going skipping with the girls, are you? They didn't have many illusions about us. But Amjad's Mum – she still thought he was a well-behaved little boy. He'd never tell a lie. So when we all showed up one morning while he explained that we wanted to borrow her clothes-line for a five-day Test Match she naturally assumed he was telling the truth – and of course he was. Except that she meant one of our street games – and that we were using it for a boundary-rope. 'You boys,' she smiled, patting Amjad on the head and making him blush to the roots of his hair. 'You have to have things just so, don't you?'

When Thursday came we left home early. We still had this idea that you had to dress up for cricket, and in any case it was a big deal for us, a huge deal, so we decided to put on our best clothes. I wore a nice new pair of loafers, a freshly ironed white shirt and a pair of smart black trousers that my Mum had bought me for weddings and special occasions. What could be more special than this, I reasoned, as I admired myself in the mirror in Mum's bedroom. Then, when she was hanging out the washing in the garden, I tip-toed downstairs and slipped out the front door. She'd have gone mad if she'd seen me dressed up like that. She wasn't like Amjad's Mum, no way. She would have grilled me. And trust me: she had ways of making you talk.

I met up with the others and we hurried on down to Muntz Road and made for the bus stop. We still didn't have a proper plan. To tell the truth, we'd probably have settled for just seeing the ground, being close to where it was all happening. And at first it was enough for us just to see all the people walking towards the gates with their picnic hampers and umbrellas – fathers with sons, groups of young men, elderly couples with shopping bags full of food and drink. There were newspaper vendors, programme sellers, fast-food stands, drinks, sun-hat merchants, one or two touts selling tickets.

There really was something special about this. You could feel it in the air. For the first time in my young life I was seeing groups of Asian men and boys heading towards a sporting event. When we used to hang around St Andrews we never saw another dark face, maybe just the odd West Indian youth with a bunch of white mates. But a Punjabi? At football? No way. The first time I actually got in the ground – sneaking in to see the last 15 minutes of a match after

CHAPTER 3 : PASSAGE TO EDGBASTON

they'd opened the gates to let people out – that was when I saw the skinhead gangs and heard them shouting and swearing about fucking black bastards and suchlike playing for the opposition.

But today it was a mixed crowd – black, brown and white together. There were even people flying the green and white flag with the crescent moon and the single star. Happy, laughing people, everywhere you looked. On their way to a great big party.

That's when we decided we had to be a part of it. We simply *had* to get in the ground.

'But how?' Amjad and Parvaz were looking at the shirt-sleeved policemen, the narrow turnstiles set in the walls, the main gates swinging open to let a big expensive car glide through and then closing behind it. The only answer I had was, 'There's got to be a way.' Last season a gang of us had managed the impossible and got into St Andrews for the local derby against West Brom, climbing over the barbed wire at the top of the fence. Surely if we could do that we weren't going to be stumped by a cricket ground? They didn't have police dogs round a Test match arena, did they? Cricket was a gentlemen's game. We were street-wise kids. And besides, we had Amjad's rope.

We needed to think. We wandered into Calthorpe Park, maybe three minutes from the City End entrance – so near yet so far. We were throwing stones into the canal, racking our brains for an idea.

'I know!'

'What?'

'We'll follow the canal.'

'Where to?'

'Well, look – it goes past the ground. Maybe we can find a way in through the fence. Somewhere where nobody can see us. There's too many people round this end.'

In fact the Grand Union misses the ground by some distance, but as we hurried along the bankside we found a place where another canal branched off – more like a drain, I suppose – and seemed to head in the direction we wanted to go. Trouble was, we had to climb down a narrow, slimy passageway to get to the drain – and already our clothes were getting splattered with muck.

The ditch we were now on did lead to the ground, but although it was only a few hundred yards long it took us half an hour to make it, the pathway was so narrow and slippery. The water in the ditch wasn't that deep – but it was deep enough to drown in, and it stank. The greasy surface was littered with tyres, cement bags full of garden rubbish, beer-cans, part of a dead crow.

'Here we are. Didn't I tell you?' We'd reached the perimeter fence. Above the hum

CHAPTER 3 : PASSAGE TO EDGBASTON

of the city we could hear the hubbub of the crowd inside – and as we stood there, panting, sweating, gagging for a drink, I thought I heard the distant 'tonk' of bat hitting ball, followed by clapping.

'That'll be England batting.' Amjad said.

'How d'you know?'

'Cos if it was us they'd be shouting and letting off fireworks, dummy.' He'd seen highlights from a Pakistan-India game on the telly, and he'd never stopped going on about it.

'Come on, all we got to do is get up there,' I said.

'Is that all?' Parvaz was looking up an almost perpendicular bank of earth topped by a solid wooden board fence, with a tree growing out the bottom of it.

'Give me the rope!' I wasn't going to be beaten now, not after we'd come all this way. Looping it over my shoulder I clawed my way up the bank, grabbing a root here, a tuft of grass there, got to within an arm's length of the tree, and slithered back down.

'See? There's no way.'

'That was a trial run. You never heard of that?' This time I set my stall out, aiming at a sturdy branch that angled out over the canal. Once I had hold of that I was able to swing my way, monkey-style, to the bottom of the fence and tie the rope round the tree-trunk. Then I slid back down it to where the others were waiting.

'Easy, see?'

'Yeah, now all we got to do is bust the fence down.'

Parvaz had a point. When all three of us had hoisted ourselves up the rope we realised this was going to take time. There were one or two slits between the boards, and we could see through to the walkway that ran round the ground and behind the stands. Good job we could, really, otherwise we might have started banging away at the fence right behind a copper. Peering through the slit we could see a pair of them standing there. Every few minutes it was 'Yes sir, right through there,' or 'This way, madam.'

Amjad was wiggling away at a board: it was loose okay, but what it needed was a damned good kick. 'We can't bust through with them standing there,' he moaned. 'We'll get arrested.'

'Just wait. Wait till something happens.' And sure enough I was right. A few minutes later came the sound of the ball being hoiked to the boundary, an eruption of cheering, and the coppers were all ears. 'Sounds like some bugger's having a go,' one of them said, and they both hurried forward to see what had happened. Time for us to dish out a bit of stick ourselves – to the fence.

CHAPTER 3 : PASSAGE TO EDGBASTON

It took us almost till lunchtime, but we made it. We finally had a board out, and a gap just big enough for us to squeeze through. Once again it was a matter of waiting for the big hit or the fall of a wicket. Then one of us would pop through while the others put the board back into position. When we were all safely inside we wedged the board back into place and headed towards the terraced rows of seats.

'Wow, look at that. It's half empty.' We dashed forward and sat down; then tried another seat, and another, and finally made our way over to where the main body of Pakistani supporters were standing with their flags and banners, singing and chanting as Imran – the princely, handsome Imran, the finest all-rounder in the world – ran in to bowl.

We saw most of England's first innings that day, and we were riveted. Here were the guys we'd watched on the telly, guys we pretended to be day in day out when we played in the street, right there before our very eyes, in the flesh. Guys like Javed Miandad, Zaheer Abbas, Wasim Raja, Abdul Qadir, fielding and bowling against giants of the English game like Lamb and Gower, Gatting and Greig, not to mention those superheroes of last year's amazing comebacks against Australia: Ian Botham and Bob Willis, in the flesh.

As the afternoon wore on it became apparent that England were gaining the upper hand. By mid-afternoon they were cruising at 220 for 5 with Gower and Geoff Miller among the runs. But then, to a terrific cheer, back came Imran for another spell, steaming in like a man possessed to rip through the tail amid wild celebrations and waving of flags. 272 all out, with Imran first off the field, his face lit up by the weary smile of a man who'd earned his 7 for 52 the hard way.

It was a fantastic day – and even when it was over it wasn't over. We should have been heading for home, and a sound ticking-off: we knew that. But what's that saying? You may as well be hung for a sheep as for a lamb? So to hell with it, we joined the crowds of kids waiting around the back of the pavilion for the players to emerge – only to realise we'd none of us brought every schoolboy's most vital item of kit: an autograph book.

'Make sure we bring some paper tomorrow,' I said as I watched Imran and Qadir and David Gower scrawling their signatures on the backs of scorecards and photographs as the sun went down and the dusk closed in.

'We coming back tomorrow?'

'With Pakistan batting? Course we are!'

CHAPTER 3 : PASSAGE TO EDGBASTON

'You are NOT going to any cricket match tomorrow. It is forbidden.' Dad was mad, and Mum backed him all the way. A lot of parents would've given their kids a good hiding, and I knew that. But I also knew my parents were decent, gentle people and that they loved me. They were making a stand for my own good.

'We can't have you wandering off to a cricket match all by yourself. Who knows what could happen to you.'

'But I'm with my mates. We can look after ourselves.'

'And how did you manage to get the money to pay your entry fee?' Mum chipped in. 'That's what I'd like to know.' She thought she had me there, but she underestimated my powers of imagination.

'We met a nice Punjabi man – a rich man. He came from Kashmir, like us – and he said we should all stick together. He paid for us.'

In those days when I really wanted something I was prepared to lie through my back teeth to get it.

Dad was a bit more suspicious than Mum. 'I've not met many Pakistanis in this town who didn't come from Kashmir,' he mused. Then he spoke louder. 'I'll not have it. Accosting strangers... begging... coming back here way past your bedtime. Worrying your mother half to death. Tomorrow you go no further than the end of Somerville Road. Is that perfectly clear?'

'Yes, Dad.'

I respected my Dad. Truly I did. It's just that what we were doing didn't seem bad to us. It seemed innocent. We loved cricket, and were desperate to be a part of what was going on. Where's the harm in that? What was going on – the emergence of Pakistan as a top-rate cricketing nation at that time – was something that would give great pride, not only to people back there, but also to us in the inner cities. And maybe we needed it more than they did back in Kashmir. Whenever England did any good at sport we had to watch the English celebrating. In my own way I hero-worshipped the Bothams and the Willises just as I did English footballers like Tony Currie and Trevor Francis, but celebrating an England win, even against Australia, didn't feel as good as it ought to. It didn't have the feeling you get when it's your own people you're cheering on. Here was a chance to support the country of our fathers, to support guys who looked like us, spoke our language, a chance to gain some self-esteem through the achievements of Imran and Zaheer and the rest of them. A chance to bond with others of our race, not through fear – running from a bunch of skinheads – but in

CHAPTER 3 : PASSAGE TO EDGBASTON

the innocent joy of celebration. Perhaps even in victory.

Of course, I was too young to understand all this at the time, let alone articulate it. If I knew it anywhere I knew it in my guts – and in my size 4 feet that led me unerringly down Somerville Road next morning, oblivious to Dad's warning, and back to Edgbaston with a school exercise book stuffed in my pocket.

For the next four days I slipped into a pattern. Out early and back late, to ever more dire threats from Mum and Dad – and a few vocabulary lessons. I never knew there was such a word as 'incorrigible' before, but I did now. I knew it in Urdu, English and of course Punjabi, because my Dad employed a bit of all three languages in his efforts to get his message across. And when September came I would amaze my English teacher by putting my hand up and telling him that I – yes, I, that lazy little Wasim in the back row, always dreaming of cricket – knew what it meant. It meant someone like me, someone who just wouldn't do what he was told – sir.

That first Test ended in disappointment. After almost matching England's first innings total with 251, we let it slip. In their second innings we had them on the rack at 188 for 8, a lead of just over 200, and the game was on a knife-edge. But somehow they got away. Bob Taylor, the Derbyshire wicket keeper, made a battling 54, and last man Bob Willis weighed in with 28 not out to post a last-wicket stand of 79. We were gutted. Their eventual 291 all out left us to make an improbable 300-plus on a worn track. Despite Imran's heroic 65, we were all out for under 200, beaten by 113 runs.

But it wasn't all doom and gloom. I'd seen my heroes in action, got my first autographs, and even managed to persuade David Gower to let me carry his bags to the car. He took my address, and a week later a big photo of him arrived in the post with his signature across it. We'd also capitalised on our enterprise and rounded up more and more kids – as if we could stop them, once they'd listened, spellbound, to the stories we told them. For the trek down to Edgbaston on the last day there were 12 of us – and a nice profit for me, Amjad and Parvaz. We charged the new kids five pence each to get in through our secret entrance. Well, we were Asian kids, budding entrepreneurs living up to the stereotype. Our parents should have been proud of us – not that we intended to give them the chance. We made all the new recruits swear on their mother's life never to tell anyone what we were up to.

CHAPTER 3 : PASSAGE TO EDGBASTON

Things weren't as bad at home as I feared. Even at that tender age I could detect an air of resignation in Dad's voice when he harangued me once more after that final day. Maybe I was imagining it, but as I think back I know I detected a hint of pride. I'd like to think that he realised I was hooked, that I now knew what my destiny was. Because I did. That experience, every bit as much as carving my first bat in the shed at the end of the garden, cemented the idea in my mind. I was going to be a first-class professional cricketer.

If I'd known how long a road it was, and where it led, I might have listened to my mother, still trying to persuade me to look to the professions. Yes, now that I think about it, now that I've been the distance and seen what can happen to kids with stars in their eyes, how hard they can fall when it doesn't happen, I'm sure I would have listened. Then I would've carried on my own sweet way.

CHAPTER 4

The talent scout

I BELIEVE in Allah. I come from a family and a culture that places great importance on religious observance and the will of Allah. At home we always prayed, and we attended the mosque. For Muslims it's a part of our daily life. I was once privileged to be in the Pakistani dressing room before an important international match, and the last thing the team did before taking the field was to pray. It didn't surprise me at all. It certainly didn't embarrass me. It seemed perfectly normal.

But I believe in luck too. Maybe I should call it fate. Whatever it is, I will always believe it was pure luck that it happened to be my PE teacher, Pete Bolland, who came storming out of the staff-room to give me and my mates a bollocking one spring day in 1983.

I'd left Somerville Road Junior school in 1982 and started at Oldknow Road. Oldknow was just another inner-city secondary school, but it had one claim to fame. Back in the 1950s it had produced a batsman who would play 50 times for England, averaging

CHAPTER 4 : THE TALENT SCOUT

46, and represent his county for an amazing 27 years, racking up 43,000 career runs. Dennis Amiss was the man, Warwickshire the county. But at 12 years of age I don't think any of us lads had heard of him, and we still didn't know much about our home county.

Maybe we were too busy living out our own fantasies to tune in to the history of the great game. We played Test matches in the street that ran for days, sometimes weeks, and when we were at school we played games that continued through morning break, lunchtime and into the afternoon. There would be anything up to 20 different games going on all over the playground, all with bald tennis balls and bats held together with different coloured electrical tape. Sometimes our PE teacher Mr Bolland came out and played with us. We'd always get him to bat – and spend the next 10 minutes scampering after the ball, out of the yard and into the road, until he decided we'd had enough and went off to join another game – or break up a fight. With so many games going on you'd get stray balls flying across you from adjacent pitches, or kids running in to take a catch from way over the far side. That's when scuffles would break out – when you got run out because some prat from another game, another year, collided with you halfway down the pitch. It was mayhem.

This particular morning I was batting and Parvaz was bowling his fast stuff. I was determined not to get out. In my own private fantasy it was England v Australia at Sydney and I was under instructions to be there again after lunch, so I'd cut out the stroke-play and started blocking. I was concentrating hard. As Dennis Lillee sent down yet another 90mph missile, right on a length, I leaned forward and played an immaculate forward defensive stroke, and imagined the 'ockers' on the infamous Hill starting to have a go at me.

'What are you, bloody deaf?'

A familiar voice interrupted my dream. Looking up I saw Mr Bolland in his blue and white tracksuit striding across the playground towards me.

'Who sir? Me sir?'

'Yes, you – and your mate.'

'Shit!' I now saw that the playground was completely empty. The bell must've gone ages ago. 'We're gonna be late!' I grabbed my coat. Parvaz shoved the ball in his pocket and threw his sweater over his shoulders.

'Didn't you hear the whistle?'

'No sir...'

We started to head towards the classroom.

'Oi, where are you going?'

CHAPTER 4 : THE TALENT SCOUT

'We got French, sir – er, no… Chemistry.'

'Maths, you plonker!' Parvaz always knew the timetable.

'Maths sir. Got the wrong day sir.'

'I didn't tell you to go.' When Mr Bolland lowered his voice you did precisely what he said. 'Put your coat down.'

'Yes sir.'

'Now, pick up the bat. You' – he turned to Parvaz – 'give me the ball.'

That's it, I thought. He's confiscating them. Bastard.

He tossed the ball in his right hand. 'Okay, let's see if you can do that again.'

'Do what sir?'

'That stroke you just played. Go on, pick the bat up. What are you waiting for?'

He sent down a slow, looping ball. Short as I was I reached right down the pitch and blocked it with an angled bat. Killed it stone dead. Hmm, he said. And sent down another, same flight, same spot. Which I blocked again. Then a third. Same result.

'Hmm.' He tossed the ball to Parvaz and turned to me. 'Well, you may not know what day it is, but you can handle a bat.' And off he went.

'Sir, sir!'

'Yes?'

'What we going to say to our French –'

'Maths!'

'Yeah, Maths teacher – about being late?'

'Tell him you forgot what day it was.'

We got a detention off the Maths teacher, but at least Mr Bolland hadn't punished us, or confiscated our gear. We thought that was the end of it. But it wasn't. Halfway through our lunch break he appeared again, walking thoughtfully across to where we were playing, standing there at square leg for a moment before crooking his finger at me. A dozen pairs of eyes followed me as I marched across the playground in silence, assuming the worst.

He took me into the changing-room and sat me down on a wooden bench. 'Who's been coaching you?' he asked.

'Nobody.' I thought he was going to say I was doing it all wrong.

'Where do you play?'

'In the street, sir.'

'And have you ever watched cricket at all?'

'Yes sir – on the telly, and sometimes me and my mates go to Edgbaston.'

'Expensive hobby,' he said with a grin. He must've known we never paid, but he didn't say anything. He reached into his top pocket and pulled out a folded sheet of paper.

'Look at this.' At the top of the page I saw the words Warwickshire County Cricket Club, but before I had a chance to see what it said

CHAPTER 4 : THE TALENT SCOUT

he was reading it to me. 'They want to know if there are any youngsters at Oldknow who might benefit from training with their under-13s.'

I just stared at him. Training at Warwickshire? Wow.

'I'm thinking of putting your name forward. I reckon they'd be interested in seeing what you can do.'

So, he was like a... a talent scout. Yes, that was it. He'd discovered me. And now I was going to be play for Warwickshire and I'd score loads of runs and get picked for England, just as I'd dreamed. And then everyone would know I wasn't just a scrawny kid with his head in the clouds...

'Mum! Dad!' I burst through the front door, threw my bag on the hall floor and hurtled into the living room. Dad was in his chair, smoking a cigarette and reading an air-mail letter. Mum was by the ironing board folding up clothes.

'Mum! Dad! Guess what? Mr Bolland says I can go and play for Warwickshire under-13s after school and then I'll go through the under-16s and under-19s and then the first team and that's how you get in the England team.'

No answer. All I could hear was my own heart thumping and the clatter of brooms as Mum put the ironing board away.

'He's their talent scout, see, and he goes around looking for future stars and that, and he picked me out and that's how it works.'

Still no answer.

I could see now that Dad was looking upset. Normally if he was at home when me and my sister got back from school he'd be pleased to see us. He'd want to know about our day. He might have a few sweets for us. But today he sat there in his chair holding this letter, and I could see his eyes were moist.

My mother gathered up the clothes she had folded and went towards the stairs. 'It's from Bhimber, from your uncle Aftab,' she said.

My father put the letter down and greeted me. 'You know, son, when I was young – about your age I suppose – my friends and I would sit under our favourite tree and look out over Bhimber and talk about how we would spend the rest of our days in the town, and grow old there. Die and be buried there. We loved our homes, you see. And now....'

I knew he had left a lot of friends, and family, behind him. And that many of them wished they could join him in the UK. I knew too that he'd come over, on his own, not because he didn't like home, but for the opportunity to better himself and provide

CHAPTER 4 : THE TALENT SCOUT

for Mum. And for us kids when we came along. And I knew that there was sadness in him whenever he got a letter from home.

But he never allowed himself to stay gloomy for long, and even though I was now past the age where he would bet me 5p that I couldn't wrestle him to the ground – as his father had done with him years ago – he would always try to be cheerful with us. He folded the letter, put it back in its envelope and wiped his eye with the back of his hand.

'What were you saying, son? Tell me what you're so excited about.' I told him it all again, slowly. I didn't get much reaction, though. What did Warwickshire County Cricket Club mean to a man from Kashmir whose idea of success was to see his son get a white-collar job rather than eking out his days – and nights – working 10 and 12-hour shifts in a bread factory? I don't think he realised what it meant to me at the time.

And next day came another reminder of life's harsh realities, when Mr Bolland caught me fighting in the playground and gave me three good whacks with his size 10 Adidas trainer.

But a few days later a letter arrived at the house, addressed to my parents. It was an official invitation to attend the training school, and it came, like Mr Bolland's letter, on headed stationery. This time Mum and

Dad realised that something important was in the air. People from their part of the world have a great respect for written documents, especially on official-looking paper, and here was one which mentioned me by name. Wasim Khan. To attend the indoor nets at Edgbaston.

It wasn't so much what Dad said as the look of real pride spreading across his face as he read the letter and then re-read it word by word to my Mum – just before I grabbed it from him, skimmed through it and ran off into the street waving it in my mates' faces. Most of them were thrilled for me. Most, but not all.

'You won't get anywhere. They're just taking the piss.' Aftab was a couple of years older than the rest of us, and a crap cricketer. He was also a smart-arse. His Dad had decided he was going to be a lawyer when he grew up, and you just knew he'd be perfect for the job. He always had an answer for everything.

'What do you know, you fat bastard?'

'They just want to get a couple of tame Asians on board to make it look good. Like they care about the community and that.'

'Who says?'

'My Dad says. He says we're here to do their dirty work and then we can all go home again. Anyway, what makes you think you

CHAPTER 4 : THE TALENT SCOUT

can make it? That's Warwickshire, man. They're looking for top cricketers, not skinny little wannabes.'

There were always one or two people like that trying to squash you. I soon learned to ignore them. Later, when Pete Bolland showed up at the house in his Mini to talk to Mum and Dad and take me to my first Tuesday evening session, half the neighbourhood 'just happened' to walk by. Our community had enormous respect for teachers, and it made us a bit special in everyone's eyes to have him round. Except Aftab, of course, who told everyone I must be in deep shit to be getting a visit from the school.

When I walked into the indoor school at Edgbaston that first session, it was like entering a foreign country. Everyone was white. And that was unnerving because to be honest, confident as I was of my ability, and cocky with it, I'd never really been anywhere where I wasn't surrounded by my own people. I'd always felt safe. Even at school, which was a good 50 percent Asian. And these guys were turning up in Range Rovers in their smart school uniforms and changing into Warwickshire sweaters and nicely pressed creams. I was wearing a pair of trousers that Pete had fished out of the games bag at school, an ordinary white school shirt, and a sleeveless V-neck pullover that my Mum had knitted. Sound enough gear, but not exactly a fashion statement. These white guys cut a bit of a dash, striding confidently around the shiny green floor, gliding in to bowl in the nets alongside coaches like Neal Abberley, Steve Rouse and Alan Townsend.

Well, I thought, I ain't going to impress them with my wardrobe. I'll have to do it with my bat.

I don't think my arrival had caused much of a stir – just a few curious glances, as if to say 'who's this kid then?' but as I started cracking the ball about the place, or defending my wicket with a broad solid bat, people started peering across to my net, and one or two even stopped what they were doing to stand and watch. Far from being embarrassed by the attention I loved it, and turned on the style, adding a little flourish to my follow-through – and getting away with it. This is what I was, a performer; and this is what I wanted, to show people just how good I was.

When the trial was over, the coach, Neal Abberley, came across to where Pete and I were standing. 'Well, you're right, Pete,' he said. 'He was worth a look, wasn't he? Can he come back for the rest of the winter?'

There was no question about that. I would have walked naked through the pouring rain

CHAPTER 4 : THE TALENT SCOUT

if they'd asked me to. Not that such extremes were necessary – although at first I did have to make the journey alone, in all weathers, and that was daunting enough. Pete had given me a lift that first time, but he had other commitments; and Dad couldn't help: he was working overtime at the factory. In any case it was still a year or two before he bought his little blue Audi. So it was the number 8 bus to Matthew Boulton college, and the 45 along Pershore Road or, if I was early, I saved a few pence by running the mile-and-a-half, timing myself on my Space Invaders watch and trying to beat my personal best. Later on, as one or two of my mates joined the scheme – Amjad, then Parvaz – we'd travel together and the journey became something to look forward to, more of an adventure.

CHAPTER 5

Handling cutlery, and other useful skills

THINGS went well for me at the indoor school, and I was soon playing for the under-13s. That following summer – or was it the one after? – I was asked to be a ball-boy when England played India at Edgbaston. It felt like a great honour, and I'm sure I must have been over the moon, but all I remember of it now was walking into the attendants' area to fetch something or other and spotting Graham Dilley in there. Graham Dilley! The guy who batted at the other end when Botham destroyed the Australian attack at Headingley in 1981. But the scales soon fell from my eyes. He was sitting there in his tracksuit, legs crossed, following the game on the telly, and smoking a cigarette.

The following season, when Neal Abberley called me into his office and said he wanted me to captain the side, I nearly burst with pride. It wasn't particularly about me being a good tactician, simply that he'd been thinking what I knew: I was the best

CHAPTER 5 : HANDLING CUTLERY, AND OTHER USEFUL SKILLS

player. Well, best batsman, I suppose. Amjad, with his left-arm chinamen, was the best bowler. No doubt about that.

However, before I could take over as captain there were a few things I needed to know, and the man to show me was Pete Bolland. It can't have been easy for him, but he had no choice. He showed me into a room and sat me down at a small table.

'You know what this is?'

On the table were a knife and fork, a spoon, and a plate. 'Yeah.' What did he think I was, stupid?

'Well, as captain of the side people are going to look to you to set an example. It's time you learned to use the old eating-irons.'

He was right. I needed to learn. At home we ate the traditional way, with chapattis and fingers. Whenever I tried eating with cutlery it was like an Englishman with chopsticks – only noisier. And he had a few more things to teach me, like how to greet people and shake hands, how to make sure I always looked smart – that sort of thing.

As cricket took over my life, and as more of my mates joined the club – Parvaz was next with his quick, whippy bowling – my school-work suffered. Don't get me wrong: it was never that great to start with, but now I had a group of mates who were all up there with me, and what we were doing – living breathing talking eating sleeping cricket – seemed normal to us. I mean, look at us – we were doing great! Weren't we?

When my Dad started reading my school report back to me it was as if he was suddenly rousing me from a beautiful dream – by pouring cold water all over me.

'*Could do better. Would benefit from spending less time talking and more time listening. Very immature for his age.* Wasim, son, this is not good. Maybe you need to spend less time on your cricket and more time with your books.'

Luckily for me, Pete Bolland came to the rescue. He didn't mean to, but he did. It was one Friday towards the end of April 1984, an evening I would never forget. The phone rang and Mum answered. She looked very serious – awestruck would be more like it – as she handed it to me. 'It's some *ghora* for you – some English man,' she said. I'd never had a phone call before. Once or twice I'd been asked to say a few words to an uncle or a cousin calling from Pakistan, but nobody had ever called me. We kids didn't call each others' houses in those days. Hardly any of my mates had phones anyway.

'Hello.'
'Wasim?'
'Ye-es?'

CHAPTER 5 : HANDLING CUTLERY, AND OTHER USEFUL SKILLS

'Wasim, it's Mr Bolland.'

'Yes sir?'

'I was wondering – are you free over the weekend?'

'Yes sir, I think so sir.'

'Good. I'd like you to do me a favour.'

'Yes sir?'

'How'd you like to come and try out for my club side?'

'Smethwick?' I glanced at Mum and Dad as they mouthed the word 'Smethwick' to each other, looking puzzled.

I wanted to grab my gear, dash out of the house, tell everyone in the street, and go there right now. Smethwick played in the Birmingham League. It wasn't an under-14 outfit; it was grown-ups, and they had a club pro. This would be a real step up. Fancy playing at the same club as Mr Bolland. I took a deep breath, and answered as casually as I could. 'Yes sir, I think I could manage it.'

I was the first of a whole stream of Asian kids that Pete Bolland drafted into the Smethwick ranks over the next few years. Parvaz followed me, then came Akhlaq, Shahid and several others, including Amjad of course. Amjad was a phenomenon. When we were little he was out there with us all the time, but as the years went by he didn't play in our street games so much. He'd get home from school and go straight to the mosque to recite the Koran off by heart. We'd all done that, from the age of about seven. It was Azeem's Dad, Malik Fazal, who taught us, in his sitting room. Four o'clock till six, Monday to Friday. It was hard work, enlivened mainly by the fact that Mr Malik had his television in there. He was a big Laurel and Hardy fan, and about 5.20pm he'd put the telly on for reruns of those old black and white films. Charlie Chaplin, Harold Lloyd, all that stuff. There we'd be, following the Urdu script with our fingers, frowning with concentration, and suddenly he'd shout out, 'Look out, you idiot, he's behind you!'

But while we laboured unwillingly, and called out 'uncle, uncle' to remind him it was time for his funny films, Amjad was taking it all in. Soon he was studying until eight at night. By the time he was 17 he could recite the entire Koran, by heart, in Arabic. After his stint at the local mosque he'd go home and do his homework, so there's no way he could have practised like the rest of us did. But he couldn't half bowl. Left-arm leg spin. That's real talent, and he had it in spades. To think he did all that and went on to play for Worcestershire.

CHAPTER 6

How many cricketers can you get in a Mini?

SMETHWICK was a whole new experience. When I first went there they had three or four West Indian players, but only one other Asian – a guy called Liaqat Zaman, known to everyone as Lockets. He was about four or five years older than me. The rest were white guys. They had an attractive ground in the borough of Sandwell with a bowling green next to it, about a 40-minute car ride away. The only thing I didn't like about it was that all the white guys had real broad Black Country accents, which sounded quite alien to me. A lot of people imagine that if you've played county cricket, the club scene is a bit of a come-down; but they're missing the point. Club cricket is the heart of the game. Smethwick had one or two genuine characters playing for them, the sort of guys who make the game what it is: fun. Carlton Green was a left-arm spinner. He was a West Indian, and to us boys he seemed as old as the hills. I think he was about 55, and still as eager as lads a quarter of his age. Whenever he hit a batsman's pad he'd spin around, stretch out a hand to the umpire, and lean back, eyes closed, head tilted as far as it would go, beseeching the heavens. Then there was our President Norman Downs, a real club stalwart who'd played for 50 years. Whenever someone made a decent score or took a few wickets he'd be there at the gate as they made their way back to the pavilion, stuffing a tenner or a 20 pound note into your pocket. The guy was a legend in his own lifetime, and it was a sad day when he passed away in 2003. We also had a system of visiting overseas players, usually an Aussie, so there was plenty of chance for a youngster to get an all-round education in the game. In fact, we learned from Pete that Smethwick had had one or two genuine stars over the years. The great England bowler S.F. Barnes was still playing for Smethwick when he represented his country back in Edwardian times. John Jameson, a prolific Warwickshire opener in the 1960s, played for us, and a little while later Aussie legend Steve Waugh turned out for the club a couple of times.

To start with, I was pretty much in awe of the old hands. I'd sit in the pavilion, scarcely daring to breathe, listening to these big old guys talking about going back to their jobs

CHAPTER 6 : HOW MANY CRICKETERS CAN YOU GET IN A MINI?

on Monday, and how they'd solve The Economy, whatever that was. They seemed super-intelligent, intellectual giants. All we boys ever talked about was how to get hold of new pair of Adidas trainers, or how we'd scrumped a load of apples from some garden down the road. These first-team guys, they were head and shoulders above us in every department.

On a Saturday we lads would play for the third XI – mostly with grown men – while Pete played in the firsts; but on Sunday he'd captain 'his boys' against lower league teams like Wombourne and Penn – so that he could keep a close eye on our development. They were friendly fixtures – except that the word friendly didn't feature in Pete Bolland's vocabulary, as we soon found out. We arrived at Wombourne with a team containing nine Asians. We looked at the opposition as they took the field. They were just a bunch of hicks. We'd show them how to play cricket. By this time I was full of myself. I'd gradually got better kit, and I had my first of pair of boots. They were monsters, the sort of thing Harold Larwood would've been proud of. God, they were ugly! But... they had spikes. That was what mattered. They felt like the real thing. We'd chosen to bat on a good wicket, and after 15 overs had amassed the grand total of... 27

for 7. PB went ballistic, stormed out to bat at number 10, knocked up a quick 50, then came back in and really tore into us. 'You think you fucking know it all, don't, you? You think all you've got to do is go out there and flash the old blade and they'll roll over and die. The difference between them and you is that they've got something to prove. You know what it is?' Nobody dared answer. 'They want to show you buggers that for all your so-called "class" you haven't got the stomach for an old-fashioned fight. They'll be down the pub tonight telling their mates that these Asian kids haven't got the bottle. And you know what?' We knew what was coming. 'They're right. You just rolled over and died, didn't you?'

What made PB such a good coach was that he'd encourage you all the way, but when you needed a bollocking he'd deliver it. He didn't pull his punches. He believed that you learned your trade the hard way, from the bottom up, and that worked for me. That first season he played me way down the order, whereas I naturally thought I should be opening. It came to a head one Saturday after a game against some village team out in the country. I'd ended up 27 not out, and was feeling frustrated because I knew I could've gone on and scored shed loads of runs. After we'd all piled into the team's

CHAPTER 6 : HOW MANY CRICKETERS CAN YOU GET IN A MINI?

minibus and set off back to Small Heath, I tackled PB.

'I can't see me scoring many runs this season, Pete.'

'Why's that then? Losing your grip?'

'Cos I'm always gonna be not out, aren't I?'

'Why's that, Waz?'

'Cos you always stick me down at number eight.'

There was a squealing of brakes and everyone in the bus lurched to one side as PB swerved into a lay-by. He switched off the engine, swung round in his seat, and let me have it in front of all my mates.

'So number eight isn't good enough, is it? Listen, you ungrateful little twat. You're playing for Smethwick for one reason and one reason only. Because I think it'll be good for your cricketing education. Not good for the club – because the club wants fighters. I can get a dozen to take your place this evening if I make a few calls. No sweat. Birmingham's full of kids like you who can "play a bit". But that's not what I'm interested in. I want kids who have the dedication and discipline to make the grade. All the way to the top. Let me tell you something, sonny. When I started out at this club they put me at number 10. Not for a week or two, not for a season or two, but for four years. Four years. That's a quarter of your lifetime, coming in with one wicket to fall. I had more last stands than General fucking Custer.'

Everyone except me was laughing. I was wriggling down in my seat so that I didn't have to look into his eyes.

'And for some stupid reason I decided to go against my own judgment and let you in at eight. Now, what are you gonna do? Take what you've got, shut your mouth and be glad of it, or whinge and whine until I shut it for you?'

PB was right, of course, and he had every right to lambast me. He put in hours, days, weeks, of his time ferrying us younger ones about in his car or the school minibus, and all for the love of cricket. People like him are the real sporting heroes when you think about it – but they have to stand back when the job's done and watch their protégés get the acclaim, and I don't think they mind one little bit. The thing is they love cricket, and they care about youngsters. They know just how easily kids can be tempted away from the discipline and disappointments of the sport by the easy distractions like gangs and drugs and alcohol. His outburst was what I needed. I finished that season averaging 40.

I should add that club cricket wasn't all deadly serious. Games are meant to be enjoyed, after all, and we certainly had our

CHAPTER 6 : HOW MANY CRICKETERS CAN YOU GET IN A MINI?

share of fun. In one of the first games I played the opposition bowler must have taken pity on me, scrawny young thing that I was. He sent down three or four gentle little lobs, all of which I whacked over the boundary rope. He muttered a curse, marked out his full run and then let me have it. Then there was the time we were playing at Four Oak Saints in Sutton Coldfield, a ground which had a wood nearby. Growing up in the inner city it seemed like a jungle to us and we couldn't wait to explore. Well, why not? We were batting, everything was going smoothly. We had time to spare. Of course, city kids that we were, we got 50 yards in and lost our bearings in a maze of trees and undergrowth. By the time Paul Vaness our skipper that day rousted us out he'd had to declare the innings closed, having run out of batsmen!

We didn't always travel in the bus. More often we piled into PB's Mini. Don't ask me how we did it, but we once travelled to a game with at least six of us plus the kit crammed in there – although a few years later when I was reminiscing with PB he swore he'd got all 11 of us in. I don't remember – and he prefers not to. As he said, if he tried that today he'd be arrested. I know in that particular game he made damned sure we batted second, and as each of us was dismissed he gave us the bus fare and told us to make our own way home.

Actually, as we kids got more confidence, and as new youngsters arrived on the scene, we started taking the bus to the ground for home games. It was a bit of a schlep, sure it was, but it was also a bit of time out to enjoy ourselves and learn a bit of independence. And it was cheap enough, once we'd learned to use a day-trip ticket to best advantage. While one of us flashed the pass and ran upstairs, the next in line would ask the driver some stupid question about a day return to Wolverhampton. Meanwhile the guy on the top deck would open the window and throw the pass out for the others to use. With the money we saved we could all call at the chippy on the way home.

Life was good. I was putting all my energies into the thing I loved best. The authorities – in the shape of my teacher PB – were on my side. And although I couldn't really talk to Mum and Dad about the game, they did their best to understand my passion. Dad would sometimes come and watch me in the nets, or in a game if he was off work. He couldn't offer any advice on my technique, but if he saw me struggling he'd put it down to my kit, or my bat, and somehow find the money to buy me something better. One time when he was

CHAPTER 6 : HOW MANY CRICKETERS CAN YOU GET IN A MINI?

watching me batting for Smethwick I set off for an easy single, but because I was wearing a set of over-sized pads I stumbled and was run out. He saved up and bought me a pair that fitted.

The only serious worry my parents had, apart from my schoolwork, was that I was losing weight. In our culture, if you aren't 15 stone and eating like a horse they think there's something wrong with you – or with your mother's cooking. I loved food, and I loved my mother's curries and sweet puddings, but I was always on the run, from school to practice or an after-school game, then off to a Saturday fixture, another on Sunday, and back to school for Monday morning. By the time I got home I was often too knackered to eat a proper meal.

That apart, though, things were going well. I was on target to fulfil my life's ambition and become an international opening bat. Of course, the minute you think you're on top of life, that's when everything's liable to turn upside down.

CHAPTER 7

Losing Dad

DAD was calling my name. It was bedtime. Past bedtime, really. I don't know why I was still awake, because when I looked at my watch it was 11.30 and I had school the next day, but I can't remember anyone waking me up, just hearing Dad's voice from his bedroom. He was calling us – me and my sister. It seemed strange that he would do that. Perhaps I had been asleep after all, and it was a dream. But there it was again. Not like he was shouting or anything, just calling our names. When I went in to see him he just said he'd been feeling sort of anxious.

'What are you anxious about?' Mum asked him. 'What's so important that you get these two out of their beds?'

'That's all right, Mum,' my sister said. 'I was reading anyway.'

'Maybe it's just my indigestion.' Dad winced as he spoke and put his hand to his stomach. 'But it feels worse than usual.'

'You've been getting that a lot recently. You shouldn't have had so many of those pakoras at supper-time. You know how it upsets you.'

CHAPTER 7 : LOSING DAD

He laughed. Mum's pakoras were one of his favourites. 'Yes, but you know what I'm like.'

'You'll never learn, will you?'

I yawned. What was this all about? Mum looking at him and smiled, but Raheena seemed worried. 'I'm going to call the doctor,' she said, as Dad winced again.

'No no – it'll pass. Maybe I should stretch my legs,' Dad said, getting up off the bed and starting for the door. He never made it. With no warning, no cry of pain, nothing, he just keeled over and lay on the floor.

All I remember of what happened next was Mum pulling on his shoulder and me helping to turn him over so that we could see his face – and the shock that went through me. He'd turned blue.

The rest is just bits and pieces in my mind. Suddenly Raheena was on the phone, shouting, and a minute later the house seemed full of people: my uncles, the doctor, the neighbours. I must've gone downstairs, and I just stayed there, not even thinking, leaning with my back against the wall in the front room. I couldn't bear to go upstairs again, not to see my Dad like that. He was going to die; I knew it, and there was nothing I could do about it, so rather than listen to the shouting and tears from the bedroom I ran into the street. It was past midnight now, but I knocked on doors and told everyone my Dad was dying, right now. I just knew it. The house filled up with more people, rallying round, trying to help, and as each new visitor came I just pointed them upstairs to where the doctor was doing everything he could – which was nothing. There was nothing to be done. My Dad had had a massive heart attack, and at 49 his life and his dreams of retirement in Kashmir were over.

*****

I'm on the plane, and we're floating above the clouds. I've watched the sun set and now it's starting to get dark. Mum is on one side of me, Raheena on the other. Nobody's said anything. It's the 17th of April. Dad died 24 hours ago. In the seats opposite us are my Dad's half-brother Uncle Khizar, and Mum's brother, Uncle Arif, the head of our family. I think they're sleeping. I can't. I don't want to, even though I've not slept for almost 48 hours now. I think I'm enjoying the peace at last. No, not enjoying it, because you can't enjoy anything at a time like this, but I'm relieved – that's the word – relieved that the pandemonium, the coming and going at the house, the crying and the grief, then the drive to Heathrow and the formalities with the body, that it's over at last.

CHAPTER 7 : LOSING DAD

Now I know I must have slept after all, because the engines have quietened down and we're descending into Islamabad.

Once we're through customs there's a whole crowd of people there to meet us: two more of Dad's brothers, and maybe a dozen other relatives or friends. They're talking to me in Punjabi – fast, excited talk, with lots of questions – and although I can follow what they're saying I can't get out a reply. My brain just won't work quickly enough, the heat is stifling me, but my feet are following them as they carry the coffin – carry Dad's body – into a big car and we pile into another one and follow them all the way to Bhimber, four hours away to the south-east.

Dad had talked a lot about the old country, but nothing he'd told me really prepared me for what I saw. Some of my mates had been out too, and they'd said it was a great place, full of familiar faces – people like us, they meant; and above all it was safe. Nobody was going to shout at you in the street, Pakis Go Home! Even so, I think I was expecting to see a primitive country, and although we did pass bullock-carts and people on foot in traditional costume driving goats or sheep along the highway with over-laden mopeds weaving in and out of them, what struck me was the things that seemed no different from home, like the grey tower-blocks, not much different from the ones in Birmingham, it seemed. The mosques, however, were spectacular: we passed a couple of huge ones, ultra-modern in their design. But these were just fleeting impressions along the way. Really, I was still stunned after all that had happened. I wasn't really taking it in. Back home my mates would be going from class to class, having lunch, preparing to play cricket after school, and people would be asking 'Where's old Wasim today?' and they'd be saying, 'Oh, didn't you know? He's over in Kashmir, burying his father.' It still didn't seem real.

We got to Bhimber in the afternoon, with the sun high in a cloudless sky. It was hot, very hot, it was dusty and the air smelled of sewage. The town was surrounded by mountains which seemed to close it in. There was no wind that day. We entered Dad's old house, where we were to stay, through a pair of little iron gates, and all of a sudden, after the trauma of the last 48 hours, it felt as though we were at home.

The house had a peaceful feel to it. There was a walled courtyard with a brick floor, and as I looked at the hollows worn in it over the years I imagined Dad to-ing and fro-ing when he was a kid. In the courtyard was a well and around it were a number of large

CHAPTER 7 : LOSING DAD

brown clay pots full of water. That's what we drank. When we took a bath we did so right there in the open behind a little wall built for privacy. When I went inside the house I realised it was actually much bigger than our place in Birmingham. It had seven or eight bedrooms, which seemed to have been added on one at a time as the family grew. It used to belong to my grandfather, but was now occupied by Dad's two brothers and their wives and children. Over it all was a flat roof. Some nights we'd take our rickety wooden beds up there and sleep out under the stars. There was plenty of room. You could have played a game of cricket up there if you wanted.

That night I lay and listened to the crickets singing, dogs barking – sometimes just an odd one, sometimes the whole neighbourhood joining in – and now and then some guy shouting at them to shut up. But that was nothing to the noise next day. We were right in town, near a factory where they processed wool, and close to the bus station, where tin buses rattled in and out from all over the country, crammed with passengers on the inside and others sitting on the roofs or clinging to the ladder at the back.

When the funeral took place it was a massive event. Literally hundreds of people turned out. I realised that Dad was very well thought of over there; he was a sort of local hero. People asked me if I was really Raja Gulzar's son. And they'd look at me and flash their teeth and nod their heads. Yes, they could see the similarity. They seemed almost proud to meet me, and were always ready to tell me stories about my father.

Normally the funeral would have taken place in the mosque, but with so many people showing up they had it in the open air under a huge awning. It was a terribly hot day, about 40 degrees. After the ceremony, when everyone lined up to take a last look at my father, we took the body to the graveyard. There we placed the coffin in the grave, and took turns, as is the tradition, to shovel earth onto it. Then began the official time of mourning, which lasted 40 days.

During that time I got to know my father's home, and later on my mother's. I had the chance to talk to people, about England, about myself, about my father. There were two questions everyone asked me about my life back home: what grade was I studying, and what was London like. They never spoke about England, always about London, as if that was the country we lived in. They just assumed that because I came from there – London – my family was rich and had three or four cars and everything we could wish

CHAPTER 7 : LOSING DAD

for. They spoke all the time about getting sponsored to come over so that they could earn money, like Dad, and send it back to their families. There was no way they could 'make it' in Bhimber. They might survive, but they wouldn't 'get on', or get their kids into university. They couldn't see any way to improve their status and get into the professions, where the money was.

Dad had written home regularly from Birmingham, and sent money of course; and because he didn't want them to know how much it pained him to be away in a cold strange land where he felt isolated and unwelcome, he would paint a picture of a great country. Yes, everything was fine; we're okay; we're doing very well. But how many times had he told us, 'When I'm older and you and your sister are married, I'm going to go back home to live. That's my dream.' Well, he'd come back home after all – and he had been welcomed in style.

There were hundreds lining the streets when the cortege drove through town. I was amazed, and proud. I thought about all the love he'd given me – and the discipline. I thought of the time he caught me scrumping, and almost lost his temper, giving me a couple of heavy back-handers, and then coming to me later to apologise with a big hug. No wonder we loved him. And no wonder he was loved in Bhimber. They all spoke of his generosity. Half his wages went back home, and when somebody once told him that they thought it might be going to people who were milking it, he always said, 'Well, it'll do someone some good somewhere. That's all that matters; it's your intentions that matter.'

After the funeral we stayed on in Bhimber for the whole of the mourning period. Some of the time I stayed at my mother's village, three miles away up a little dirt road. It was a small place with maybe 20 families living there, including my Mum's sister. It seemed cooler there, more peaceful. I felt very much at home. Once we'd shaken the dust off our clothes – I was dressing traditional style now, for comfort as much as anything else – we would sit in the shade of the trees, and look out across the fields to the hills that surrounded us. Mum's house was on a sort of cliff-top, with a 50-foot drop around it. It was made of lightweight, worn-out brick and the walls had massive cracks zigzagging down them. There were chickens running loose and a few cows. But they were safe. There was no traffic in the village: the streets were far too narrow. Walking down one of the alleyways that connected the houses you might run into a bicycle, maybe a donkey wandering free or browsing on

CHAPTER 7 : LOSING DAD

the weeds. But that was it: anyone who came by car had to leave it out in the fields and walk the last few hundred yards.

At night you could lie on your back and see a million stars, and the whole village would be steeped in the smell of wood smoke and chapattis being baked. You'd hear the murmur of neighbours' voices as they sat and talked until two or three in the morning. Often we'd sleep out under the open sky, and if we had to go to the toilet we just trotted out into the dark fields like everyone else. It was a long, long way from Small Heath. It was quiet, it was calm, it was safe, and it was where I came from.

Gradually I started to find out more about my Dad from people I met – family, friends, even total strangers who had found out who I was and would stop me in the street to sing his praises. They said he was a good man with a big heart – but not a saint, far from it. One man told me about the first time he and Dad tried smoking. 'I think we were 12 years old, perhaps 13. We managed to scrape together a few rupees, and we decided to go to a little shop in town where they didn't know us to buy some cigarettes. Then we sneaked off into the fields and smoked the whole lot. Every one of them. Can you imagine? Twenty cigarettes, non-stop. I remember how sick I felt, but your father was in a terrible condition. Much worse than me. I think he inhaled. That was the trouble. He went home bent over double and once he started vomiting he couldn't stop. His mother had to call the doctor. They were worried to death. In the end your Dad had to own up – and his father gave him a good thrashing to add to his troubles. But he never told them who was with him, so I got away with it!'

Dad loved his father. He almost hero-worshipped him. The story is that he used to follow him around, never letting him out of his sight. One day, when he was about 10, my grandfather had to go to Lahore to find work. Lahore was a long journey – about four hours on the bus. Somehow Dad persuaded an older boy, who had a motorbike, to follow the bus all the way, with Dad perched on the back. Imagine Grandad's surprise when he got off the bus after a full morning's ride and there was his 10-year-old son grinning up at him in the street!

When I wasn't listening to stories like that I spent quite a bit of time hanging around in town, talking with the local kids. There was always a cricket game going on somewhere and after a while I decided I might as well join in. It'd be useful to get a bit of batting practice. Keep myself in shape for when I went back home. One day I was

CHAPTER 7 : LOSING DAD

watching a bunch of 12 or 13-year-olds playing with a cork ball – which is quite hard: not like a proper cricket ball but hard enough. They were just playing in their ordinary clothes. One or two were even barefoot. Nobody had boots on or anything. I was wearing my sandals. After I'd been standing there for a while I asked if I could have a bat. To tell the truth I fancied showing off. There was a bit of a crowd watching and here was a chance to put on a display for them – a sort of batting masterclass. After all, I was now a regular in Warwickshire under-15s. Might as well show them the sort of standard they should be aspiring to. I twirled the bat, took up a slightly exaggerated stance – shamelessly playing to the gallery – and then saw this blur as a young kid came tearing in and whipped in an 80-mile-an-hour yorker – which I missed completely. Pity it didn't miss me. It got me right on my bare toes. If this had been back home I'd have gone down like the proverbial sack of potatoes. It hurt like hell. Here, though, I needed to save face at all costs. Was I not Raja Gulzar's son? This amazing guy who lived in the Promised Land? As I flexed my leg and fought back the urge to yell, I had the presence of mind to look at my watch. 'Goodness,' I said, 'I was meant to be home five minutes ago,' and walked stiffly round the corner where I slumped to the ground and inspected the damaged through tear-filled eyes. Two broken toes, a split nail, and a nice splodge of blood mixed with the dust and sweat.

In some ways, what happened was no great surprise. I'd watched enough street cricket there to realise that the amount of talent hidden away in these towns and villages was quite amazing. I was genuinely shocked by what I saw. There were kids playing there in their ordinary clothes with make-do equipment who could easily have been picked up by a county youth set-up such as I was involved with back home. But of course, there was no such opportunity in Kashmir. Even then I realised what a massive stroke of luck I'd had when Pete Bolland singled me out that day. If I lived in Kashmir, forget it. That kind of miracle just wouldn't have happened.

I'd fitted in much better than I thought I would out there. Yes, my Punjabi was a bit rusty and I sometimes struggled to keep up in conversations, but it was like my mates had said: you felt safe. I was surrounded by people like me, and my extended family. I could go wherever I wanted to without fear. Nevertheless, I was starting to think about home, about my mates at school, and wondering how my life would change now

CHAPTER 7 : LOSING DAD

that I was – as everyone kept reminding me – the man of the house.

As we flew home at the end of May, I thought about the things I'd seen, about the fact that this was really the beginning of life without my father. I'd seen how my people lived out there, and I hoped that would make me appreciate what we had at home. And of course I wondered about my cricketing ambitions. Would I have to give that up so that I could look after my Mum and Raheena?

CHAPTER 8

Give Wasim the menu, he knows about this stuff

WHEN we left England I had been in the squad for the county under-15s and was preparing to play a few friendlies for Smethwick. Everything was going nice and smoothly. Now I was back; I had grieved for six weeks, I had lost weight, I had missed the start of the new season, and I had a lot on my mind. I was the man of the house. That's what everyone told me, and I took it seriously. My first priority had to be to my Mum and my sister. Cricket? Well, cricket was just a game, people were saying. It would have to take second place. But could it?

The thing was, I still had a fire in my belly, that desperate ambition to reach the top as a cricketer, so I tried to balance the pull of the game against my new responsibilities within a fatherless family. While my mates all gathered in the street to play, or just hang out in the evening, I would leave them at eight o'clock and go back home so that my mother and sister were not left on their

CHAPTER 8 : GIVE WASIM THE MENU, HE KNOWS ABOUT THIS STUFF

own. I kept that up for a few weeks, and then I started playing out a bit later, and a bit later still. Even so, when I turned out for Smethwick on a Saturday I'd rush home straight after close of play to see that everything was all right, and to keep them company. I had to: if people came by to pay their respects, then it was my duty to be there to greet them. It was expected in our community, and I wanted people to see unity and strength when they came to visit, not disintegration. I wanted too to show that I was brave, that I could take it in my stride, this being the head of the household.

In some ways, then, I was growing up fast, but not at school. For the first few weeks after coming home I was a little subdued, but it wasn't long before my old cheeky self re-emerged, full of back-chat, more eager to make my mates laugh than impress my teachers. I just didn't take education all that seriously – but then neither did most of us. On the street no one had much respect for schooling. They should have done, but they didn't. If I had been the kind of scholar who got straight As, well, big deal: not many of my peers would have been that impressed. I'd be more likely to win their approval by getting my name in the papers for making a big score somewhere. Mates like Parvaz and Amjad had little time for study either. None of us felt that we would suffer if we did badly at school. We'd get by. We'd find a job in a factory. Everything would be fine. At least we'd be making an honest living.

The sad part of all this is that I was bright enough to have done better. So too was my sister Raheena, and, unlike me, she was keen to study; but the men in the family decided that she shouldn't go on to college. It was an alien concept to them at that time. Girls had always stayed home to help their mothers. Why do anything different? Raheena was horribly disappointed, but she had no say in the matter. Only a few years later she would watch the next generation of girls in our community being encouraged to go the distance academically.

I was soon back training and playing for the under-16s – me, Amjad, Parvaz and eight public schoolboys, guys from Rugby, Solihull, King Edward's and the like. But by now I was quite used to Edgbaston, although I still got a thrill every time I walked in there. I suppose I had a sort of double-edged response to it. In many ways it was quite an alien world, full of able and self-confident white people who seemed not to have a worry in the world, but at the same time it was also a place where I felt I too belonged. After all, I had captained the under-13s: I was part of the furniture. So

CHAPTER 8 : GIVE WASIM THE MENU, HE KNOWS ABOUT THIS STUFF

each week when I was signed in by Ernie, the attendant, and smelled the special smell of the place, it was like home from home. It was a fantastic place to be. It had class. The showers were always clean and the water always piping hot; there was decent kit, and plenty of it – 30 or 40 balls just lying there casually in a box. It was a long way from the old days when we used to knock those tennis balls up on the roof and sneak back for them after school.

It was like living in a land of plenty. Everything was organised, everything was clean; the coaches were all smartly dressed and well groomed. They even had their own parking spots. They were mostly ex-players, so when they spoke you listened. These blokes had walked the walk. You respected them. The whole place had a sense of history: all around the entrance hall there were photographs of players from earlier generations – some who'd made it, some who hadn't. There was an adolescent Gladstone Small in glasses, which always made me laugh. If a gawky kid like that could make it into the England team, so could a skinny little Kashmiri from Somerville Road. Every week when I walked in I'd look at all the photos, and every week I'd renew my determination to make it to the top.

Sometimes when I got home I'd talk to the other kids about Edgbaston, and I'd make it sound even better than it was. Oh it's so huge, man, and so posh, and the coaches all drive Ferraris, man, and do you know they even have armed guards on the gate who salute you as you walk in – oh, I'm telling you man it's a fantastic place! What this said about me, of course, was that I was still in awe of the place. Occasionally I'd walk across to where you could look out onto the county ground proper, gaze at the velvety sward and wonder what it must be like to actually tread on that hallowed turf, or send a square cut skidding across it to the boundary boards.

While I dedicated myself to the game, my general apathy towards the academic side of things resulted in me leaving school in 1987 with two miserable O-levels, in English Literature and History. Like most of my mates, I went on to Josiah Mason College to resit my exams. This time I paid a bit more attention, and actually managed to get interested enough to pass in four more subjects. Then I sat A-levels in English, History and Economics, although I only managed to scrape a pass in English. I might have done better if I hadn't missed weeks at a time practising and playing and taking off on mini-tours. I distinctly remember walking

CHAPTER 8 : GIVE WASIM THE MENU, HE KNOWS ABOUT THIS STUFF

into English one day – one of two lads surrounded by 15 girls – and being asked by the teacher to introduce myself as 'a new member of our class'. And he wasn't winding me up: he genuinely didn't recognise me.

Perhaps I was growing up a bit. I was certainly gaining a little self-confidence as my experience broadened. That year Parvaz and I were selected to attend a national coaching course at Lilleshall as a result of our performances with the under-16s – one highlight of which was playing against a Yorkshire side featuring a young Darren Gough and being run out on 99.

I was also working part-time at a cash-and-carry, carting boxes around, contributing to Mum's housekeeping out of my £45 a week, and feeling a bit of pride: I was pulling my weight at last.

In 1988 I turned 17 and decided I needed more mobility. I'd learn to drive. Around where we lived the driving instructors were charging about £12.50 an hour. That was a lot of money, and despite my part-time job, I just didn't have it. So I asked Gary and one or two of the older guys where they'd learned. They sent me to a little West Indian guy who rode around in a heap of a thing held together with pop rivets, duct tape and filler. I took one look and went back to Gary. 'You cannot be serious,' I said. 'Have you seen the state of his car?' He sent me straight back and told me to ask about the guy's prices. I soon saw his point.

'Tree pound fifty, man. Plus refreshments.' Yes, refreshments. Along with your hour's tuition you got a can of coke and a bag of crisps. That's the neighbourhood for you. I learned the basics with our Jamaican friend, then polished my technique with a couple of £12.50 lessons, and passed the test first time. My uncle Arif found me a little silver VW Golf, and I was away.

At this time I was still turning out for Smethwick. It would be another year or two before I moved to Old Hill. By 1988 I was in the seconds, making my highest ever score for the club, 147 not out. By the following season I had developed a real hunger for big scores, and the ability to get them. That year, 1989, I almost – but not quite – played alongside Steve Waugh. Somerset had him and New Zealand's Martin Crowe on their books and couldn't field both overseas players, so the young Australian was often stuck in the seconds. Smethwick's President, the late Norman Downs, used his contacts with Somerset to good effect and got him a game or two with us. I would have given anything to bat alongside him, but the nearest I got was sitting in the dressing-room watching him prepare to bat.

CHAPTER 8 : GIVE WASIM THE MENU, HE KNOWS ABOUT THIS STUFF

Club cricket was in some ways more forgiving than the county version. Because you played Saturday and Sunday you had two chances most weekends to get a decent score, less time to brood if you were out cheaply on a Saturday. I was desperate to do well for the club, partly for my own sake, partly for the club's, but also to impress Neal Abberley. Every Monday when I showed up at training he would want to know how I'd got on at the weekend – although mostly he knew, from checking the scores in the *Sunday Mercury.*

We were all growing up now, moving on from our childhood escapades. My mate Akhlaq also had a car – an old Honda Accord – and we'd all pile in to make the trip from Small Heath. No more hour-and-a-half journeys on three buses; no more ticket scams; no more larking about in fish and chip shops on the way home; and no more the three or four of us scrounging lifts from the grammar and public schoolboys in their beautiful big cars and always asking to be dropped off at a suitable distance from home in case they ever saw where we lived. That was strange – probably for them as it was for us, because when we had a bat or ball in our hands we undoubtedly felt superior to all those kids, and I dare say we showed it. Once the game was over it was as if we shrank back into ourselves. They were so much better off than us, so relaxed in each other's company. It was as if there was some sort of social game going on now, and only they knew the rules.

That earlier phase, however – making our own way to training on the buses – had been an important part of our education. We'd learned to take responsibility for getting ourselves to and fro. We'd learned to value our time and make the best use of it. For me as a batsman, though, the great thing about travelling by car was I had less time to brood over a bad performance. Sometimes, if I'd played poorly, I would sit on the bus and let it get to me. Now there was far less time to dwell on it. We'd all be home in 20 minutes and diving into our evening meal.

Warwickshire didn't have an under-17s or under-18s team at this time. If you did well at under-16s, as I did, averaging over 45, the next step up was under-19s. I made my debut for them in 1987, aged just 16. I was still pretty small and certainly skinny; everyone I played with seemed bigger and stronger. But in a way that worked to my advantage as a batsman: I had to rely on skill and, above all, sharpen my timing. Even so, on slow wickets, I tended to struggle. When the ball isn't coming through there are fewer chances to flick or nudge it away,

CHAPTER 8 : GIVE WASIM THE MENU, HE KNOWS ABOUT THIS STUFF

exploiting the pace of the ball. A drive is less likely to penetrate the field. To counteract that, you try lofting the ball over the top – and of course, with my weak arms ansd slight frame it often didn't carry, so I ended up getting caught at mid-on or mid-off.

Today a county team would get the dietician to work on someone like me as I was then, and recommend the right foods to build me up. But we had no advice. Diet – and the way it can affect performance – never entered our heads. Some of the lads smoked; a lot of them drank beer – and plenty of it. At home I just ate as I always did: curries and chapattis. Nobody ever told us that we shouldn't have a square meal before a game. If it was lunchtime, we just ate, never giving a thought to how it might affect our performance. And as I started travelling with the team I relished the chance to eat hotel food, takeaways, all that stuff. After the food I'd grown up with, it seemed exotic, like forbidden fruit. Of course, at night we often ended up in some Indian restaurant, and everyone expected me to be an expert. Being the kind of guy I was, I gave them what they wanted. Actually, I knew nothing. Half the dishes I'd never heard of, and most of them in any case were just the same as my Mum made but with a bit of extra tomato or onion or something. At home, every dish we had was called curry; the only difference was whether it was lamb, chicken or lentils. But when the boys were eating out I talked them through many a menu, blinding them with science – and still do.

CHAPTER 9

At last — a contract

1989 WAS a golden summer for me. I racked up a huge number of runs for Smethwick, and for the county. There was a nice 100 out of 228 for 8 for England Schools against Wales, and in July I went south with Dom Ostler and Parvaz for the Inter-counties Under-19 festival at Oxford and Cambridge, winning our group and going on to beat Surrey in the final. We were open-mouthed at the sight of the Oxford colleges, the Gothic architecture, manicured greens and pale stone quads, the academics scurrying by in their gowns or tweeds. It was an England we'd vaguely heard of but never seen. This is where Parvaz and I first started following the lads into town at night, venturing into pubs and indulging in guilty feasts of scampi and chips. We were at Oxford, so it was only right that we got ourselves a bit of education. Beer, however, was always off the menu, and it never really interested us anyway.

There were four of us Asian lads on that tour, and of course we formed a bit of a clique. We must have put the other lads' noses out of joint at the beginning, because when we were together we naturally talked in Punjabi. We never even thought about it. We only realised what we were doing when we heard someone muttering 'talk bloody English, can't you?' Thereafter we agreed always to talk English around the other guys. We wanted to blend in, even though we though we found these public schoolboys quite alien in many ways, and a bit precious. I remember sitting in the dressing-room one day listening to two of them.

'You know I really like the grain on your bat, Simon.'

'Yes, it's super, isn't it?'

'They say the closer the grain the better the surface.'

'Yes, some bats just don't have it, do they?'

Parvaz leaned across and whispered in my ear. 'For fuck's sake, man! You ever heard anything like it?'

As the scores piled up I found myself looking at certain players who were contracted, or who were getting selected for Warwickshire seconds, and thinking, 'Hey, I'm better than that. Why not me?' That's the kind of confidence that flows through a batsman's veins when the runs are flowing. On the other side of the coin, some of my

CHAPTER 9 : AT LAST – A CONTRACT

Asian friends were still telling me I was wasting my time. We never get any recognition, they told me. Show us the Indian and Pakistani kids around the counties. There aren't any, are there? It's a white man's game.

For me, though, the jury was still out. But I was starting to wonder whether I had a future at Edgbaston. I was unsettled enough to write to two counties – Derbyshire and Hants – and ask for a trial. At first nothing happened; then the shit really hit the fan as the local paper got wind of what I'd done. 'Trials for Wasim', ran the headline on the sports page; and no sooner had that hit the streets than I was called in for a meeting with Neal Abberley. What the hell was this all about, he wanted to know. I told him that these other counties had been tapping me up. At least I had the satisfaction of seeing his concern. 'This is going to be a crucial year for you,' I heard him say. 'You did okay last year, but we need more.' There was going to be no contract yet, but if I kept on doing what I was doing there could soon be one.

In a way, this was fair enough. The first team were starting to motor. They were fifth in the Championship, with Andy Moles having knocked up 1,800 runs and Tom Moody making a big bang as overseas player, scoring 100 in 36 balls against

Glamorgan. In addition there were two other youngsters, Jason Ratcliffe and Dominic Ostler, starting to make their mark. I knew I'd have to be damned good to break in.

All I could do was get my head down and show just how good I was, and the following season, 1990, I scored over 3,000 runs in all forms of the game, including eight 100s and 15 half-centuries. By the time I'd racked up four consecutive 100s for the under-19s I was batting with total freedom. I was having a dream season, and later heard that as many as seven counties had expressed an interest in me. I was again selected for England Schools – and for once I had an 'in': Hugh Cherry, who also managed our under-19s at the time, was one of the selectors. There was no way I was going to be overlooked by him.

In June, I got a trial outing with the second XI, against Worcester at New Road in a one-day game. They fielded a hell of a team: a bowling line-up of Graham Dilley, Neil Radford and Stephen Rhodes to start with, plus a few other first-team regulars. After they'd made 230 or so in their 50 overs we got off to a horrible start: we were 87 for 4 when I went in at number six. But thanks in no small part to my 66 not out we won by four wickets, with Gareth Williamson scoring 70-odd at the other end. The then

CHAPTER 9 : AT LAST – A CONTRACT

second-team coach Mark Scott told me years later that Graham Dilley was so impressed by me that day that they discussed my performance in the dressing-room afterwards. Dilley apparently said something like 'It'll be interesting to see if this boy is allowed to play with that sort of freedom once he's been on the staff for a few years.' It was an astute comment, because as time went on I was to become a far more robotic player and lose a lot of my natural exuberance as a batsman.

In August came one of the sweetest moments of the season. We were playing Northants, and were struggling at 80-odd for 3 when I got myself going big time, and made a huge ton, 171 not out. At the end of that day's play Neal Abberley called me over and said the magic words. 'I'm going to recommend you for a full contract, Waz.' I don't think he had any choice.

This was fantastic news and I couldn't wait to get back home and tell my family, my mates and everybody else who wished me well. But my delight at the good news was tempered by the fact that old mates like Parvaz and Amjad had seen their hopes fade. So of the three of us there was only myself at this stage, although they would hang in there and later pick up contracts at neighbouring Worcestershire.

I signed the agreement with Warwickshire on the morning of 21 August. I'd no idea it was going to happen that day. If I had I would have shaved. I was down in the nets when the coach Bob Cottam came and shook me by the hand, took me up to the chief executive's office and sat me down at his desk. After I'd signed, they brought a photographer in – so the terrible little moustache I had grown that year was consigned to immortality. And so was my new signature. For some reason – perhaps hoping that one day I'd be pursued by hordes of autograph-hunters – I'd spent a lot of spare moments that year practising different styles.

My contract was for the remainder of the 1990 season plus two more years. It would pay me the princely sum of £160 a week for the remainder of the season, and the same for the following two years, each running from 1 April to 30 September. In addition there was the £12 overnight allowance for away fixtures, and 23p a mile if I used my car to travel. I still have the original contract framed and mounted in my Mum's living-room. It was never going to make me rich, but it made her very proud of her only son. When my first monthly cheque arrived I did what we were brought up to do, giving it away to my family and various community

CHAPTER 9 : AT LAST – A CONTRACT

charities. Westerners say that what goes around comes around. In the community I grew up in we have the same idea: to us, giving away your first salary cheque ensures good fortune in the future.

I was now one of 22 contracted players at my home county, all competing for a place in the first XI, but I was special. I had become one of the first British-born Pakistanis to play professional cricket. Walking down the streets of Small Heath I was now stopped by people I hardly knew and warmly congratulated. Not only were they delighted by my achievement, but they were expressing pride in such a significant step forward being taken by one of their people. I had broken through. Perhaps others would follow. It gave a little bit of hope to everyone.

Naturally, when the season came to an end I looked forward with great excitement to the following year, but first I had another adventure to occupy me. In 1989 we had had an Australian player with us at Smethwick. Brad McNamara came from Sydney, and as much as he loved to talk about the place, I loved to listen. I'd always fancied Australia, ever since the winter nights when I'd huddled under the blankets and listened to Peter Baxter broadcasting from the Test Matches Down Under, and of course I numbered among my boyhood heroes the likes of Greg Chappell, Allan Border and D.K. Lillee. Brad made everything about the place sound so exciting, and I just knew I had to go there. I talked to Pete Bolland about it and he said that not going to Oz when he had the chance was one of his biggest regrets. That clinched it for me.

My Mum was obviously worried when I told her my plans. And of course I felt bad about leaving her and Raheena on their own for six months, but at the same time I knew that I could do with some time away, partly to find myself, and partly to do some growing up. It would be good to look after myself for six or seven months rather than relying on my mother. I was ready too to taste a new environment. If you stay too long in any one place, wanting to be with your mates, all that happens is that they move on instead. And that's what was starting to happen with me. Raja was at a polytechnic in south London, Parvaz was away at college and engrossed in his studies. Amjad was busy with his Koran recitation. It wasn't the way it used to be. And to be fair, everyone around me seemed pleased, excited even, that I was going to go halfway round the world.

Once the dream started to look as though it would become a reality, I could hardly sleep at night. Cricket took second place in my imagination to the other delights of a country which offered golden sand, endless sunshine, and a population of females who would all, surely, be as good-looking as the cast of *Home and Away*. By the time I boarded the Canadian Airlines flight that would take me to the other side of the planet I was beside myself with excitement. I was also, if I'm perfectly honest, very aware that I was now going to be free of the responsibilities, and the restraints, of family. Yes, I'd miss them – but not all the time. Looking back now, I can see that I learned a lot that first trip, but very little about cricket. It was the first time I had been away, apart from a few days at a time on cricket tours. But at heart I've always been an independent person and this was a chance for me to find myself.

CHAPTER 10

Bright lights of Sydney

I WAS to play for Western Suburbs in Sydney. They were a decent outfit. In recent years they had had players of the calibre of Dave Gilbert, Greg Matthews and Dirk Welham in their ranks, all Test players. So the level of cricket was pretty high. As at Warwickshire, I felt confident with a bat in my hand, but socially I felt very unsure of myself at first. I watched, and listened, and tried to learn. In a way we Asian guys had always tended to stand back and watch how others did things, and I had become a good observer. Perhaps that's how I came to be a decent mimic later on, amusing the guys by imitating other players.

When I first arrived in Sydney I stayed in a couple of guesthouses in Burwood. That was a pretty dreary existence, and I had very little to occupy my time once practice was over. I tried to get into a daily routine, which revolved around going to the gym, coming back and watching TV, or maybe wandering around town, enjoying the scenery and atmosphere of one of the world's most laid-back cities. It was maybe 30 minutes from

CHAPTER 10 : BRIGHT LIGHTS OF SYDNEY

Burwood to the downtown area and I used to love just ambling around the waterfront in the shadow of the Opera House, but I was, essentially, lonely.

Training was on Tuesdays and Thursdays, and one of the guys would usually call by and drive me to the ground. At this stage the only social life I had was after the game on a Saturday when we'd all head for town and the James Craig, a huge restaurant with live music playing and lots of pretty girls. Then that was it until the following weekend.

But the quiet, solitary life wasn't going to last for much longer. I hadn't been in town long when I had the good fortune to be invited to stay with a wonderful family called the Burkharts whose son Peter played with me at the club. They called me their English son, and I will always remember them as my Aussie family. Not only had I now landed on my feet as regards creature comforts – it was a super house and I had a fabulous room – but Pete was the unofficial social secretary at the club. Suddenly, from being a wide-eyed stranger in a foreign land, not really knowing what to do with myself in the evenings, I was going out five nights a week.

On Sunday it was the Darling Harbour, Monday the Hard Rock Cafe. Tuesday it was Tracks at Epping, and Wednesday the Parammata Eels club, winding the week up at Cauldron in Kings Cross. Fridays and Saturdays we tried – not always successfully, I have to admit – to stay in and prepare for the weekend game. I was, I suppose, dazzled by all that I now saw. I was still pretty shy. I liked the idea of going out and meeting people, but inside I felt guilty. What would my family think of me socialising with these white guys and going into places where alcohol was served, with a bunch of guys who couldn't wait to pour as much of it down their necks as they could manage?

But the way I saw it, I was on leave. I was out in the world seeking my fortune, and after all the hard work I'd put in over the past few years I deserved a bit of fun. In any case, I was fairly restrained in the way I behaved. Let's say I observed more than participated that first year, although I did learn how to dance, and I certainly became interested in Australian girls. Here I was, surrounded by these young guys who loved partying. They played hard, on and off the field. I was staggered to see how much they drank – not so much the quantity as the fact that they could practise the next day as if nothing had happened. I found the sheer fatigue of staying out late night after night really took its toll on me physically.

They were fun times – if a little hairy. As the non-drinker it always fell to me to drive

CHAPTER 10 : BRIGHT LIGHTS OF SYDNEY

someone's car home and I had to round up some ugly sights at the end of the night. Then I'd have to concentrate on the road with a gaggle of monkeys in the back, who thought it was the wildest thing to lean forward and yank the handbrake on. I became quite adept at surviving sudden 180 degree turns, screeching to a halt, and driving off through a haze of blue smoke as if nothing had happened.

Some people go completely nuts when they're away from home for the first time. I know I never did anything really rash or dangerous, but considering I was a professional sportsman I must admit I just about lost the plot over that winter. On at least one occasion I got home from downtown at seven in the morning, grabbed a bowl of cereal and then showed up ready for a game at nine o'clock. I was a young man set loose in a beautiful country; my accommodation was all provided and the couple of hundred dollars we got every week was all pocket money. I had a crowd of new friends and right now that seemed far more important to me than cricket. Why should I worry? When I went home I had a two-year contract waiting for me. I'd cracked it.

Despite all the fun, though, I did further my cricketing education in one important way. I developed a thick skin. The whole approach to the game out there was competitive. Very competitive. They gave you plenty of flak on the pitch. They had an attitude towards us Poms, black or white, and they let you know it. I remember being startled one time when I played a ball out into the covers and set off for a quick single. My partner saw the fielder closing in rapidly and sent me back. As he gathered the ball and threw it at the stumps, the guy at cover point shouted, 'Hey Pom, just because you're dark doesn't mean you're quick, now fuck off back to your crease!'

I only once felt I was being got at because of my colour, and that time I almost lost it. We were playing a team called Campbelltown and I'd just hit their star bowler for several consecutive boundaries. Next thing, he was down the wicket in his follow-through and calling me a black bastard. It was the first and last time I have had to be restrained on a cricket field. I'd never really encountered that sort of blatant racism before and it really pushed the wrong buttons. The worst I'd had at home was the kind of back-handed compliment people pay you when they're trying to show that the colour of your skin's the last thing on their mind. 'Waz, you're a top bloke,' a teammate at Warwickshire once said to me. 'You're different from the rest of them.'

CHAPTER 10 : BRIGHT LIGHTS OF SYDNEY

In the end, that sort of experience in Sydney was good for me. It helped toughen me up a bit. Over here I feel young cricketers are still treated with kid gloves, even as young pros. We're treated too politely; not always hungry enough, and we probably play too many games. But there's no doubt in my mind that the amount of competitive cricket we play here can dull your appetite. It can actually make you less competitive in your outlook. You failed today? Well, maybe you'll score a few tomorrow. Towards the end of a season you can actually get blasé about the game. Down Under I only played once a week, so when match day came around I was determined to make the best of it.

CHAPTER 11

Living a double life

I RETURNED from Australia in the spring of 1991 ready to play my way into the first XI – and fully expecting to do so. I felt bigger, stronger – mentally as well as physically – and much more grown-up; and to prove the fact I had a little goatee beard.

But the new season didn't get off to the best of starts. I was sitting at home, telling my family about my adventures – the edited version, of course – when the phone rang. My Mum answered, and handed it to me. It was Mushtaq Mohammed, the former Pakistani Test captain.

'Where the hell have you been? Warwickshire have been trying to contact you all day.'

'Why?'

'Why? Because they started the pre-season sessions this morning, that's why. And they don't expect to have to chase around after you like a school kid. Now get yourself down here, and be quick about it.'

I had given it some thought, but it hadn't got any further than 'Hm, must call the ground some time and find out when we're due back'. I'd obviously become too laid-back in Oz. I got another bollocking when I eventually arrived at the ground, and was ready for a third from our new coach, Bob Woolmer. Bob Cottam had resigned during the winter and the former Kent and England man had taken his place. Nobody knew what to expect, so there was a bit of tension in the air. I was braced for a bit of 'what day do you call this?' but it never came. He just walked into the dressing-room, shook hands and wished me luck.

1991 was the start of what would turn out to be a long apprenticeship in the seconds. So far I'd progressed at a decent rate, and fully expected to settle in and be knocking at the door of the first team by the end of the season. If only.

One of the first differences I noticed at this level was in my own game. For the first time I became afraid of failing. There's a lot of fear in cricket, especially for a batsman. One mistake and you're out. Then the rest of the guys post a big score, you bowl the other lot out twice and your chance to make it right in the second innings is gone. It's an unforgiving game, and when things start to go against you it preys on your mind. I had always been a flair player. As I said, I wasn't strong; I relied on technique and timing. Now I realised I was in a make-or-break situation, and at the same time the coach was telling me to cut out certain shots. They were too risky. Like most of the youngsters on the staff I ended up being more afraid of what the coach would say than I was about actually getting out. We had good reason to be wary of the coaches. In 1992 we had a young lad called Ben Usher playing for us against Surrey seconds at the Oval. He was a bright kid, with a good education behind him, and very articulate. We were playing the semi-final of a knock-out competition and we basically got hammered, 90-odd all out. We knew what we were in for, and the coach didn't disappoint us. We were all a bunch of useless tossers, and what the hell did we think this was, a bloody girls' school outing, and so on and so on. We all sat there looking at the floor, and suddenly Ben piped up. 'Look, are you just going to stand there telling us everything we did wrong and making us feel small, or are we going to have a grown-up discussion about this?' He was gone at the end of the season, and no one can say they were surprised.

The pressure got to me; there's no doubt about it. That first season I was in and out of the seconds, playing 10 games, averaging a modest 25, and doing 12th-man duties in a few others, hoping at least to get on the

CHAPTER 11 : LIVING A DOUBLE LIFE

field if someone was injured. Otherwise, maybe half a dozen of us who weren't selected would practise in the nets. On the field, the best I managed that summer was a couple of half-centuries. Being uncertain of my place made every innings crucial, and this was where the fear really took hold and probably impaired my performance. I started looking to stay in rather than actually make runs. The more I experienced the pressures that applied to a young pro, the more I appreciated the achievement of the few who battle through and make it to the very top.

But it wasn't all bad. I was making friends among the other lads. There was Michael Bell, with whom I'd later spend time in Australia. He was such a laid-back guy; perhaps it was in his Caribbean genes. A medium-fast bowler who had been around the leagues for some time, he was nicknamed The Breeze. He made everything look that easy. In his younger days Belly had an Afro that a Colombian footballer from the 1970s would've been proud of. I met him in 1992 when I was playing in the Birmingham League and he was turning out for Mitchells and Butler. When he walked out to the wicket I thought 'Who's this big bloke with the silly Afro?' and started giving him a bit of banter. He stopped at the crease, turned round and said, in his broad Brummy accent, 'And who the fuck do you think you are, eh?' Later that year he showed up at Edgbaston. He had a trial with the seconds. That's when he and I became mates.

Despite outward appearances, Belly was a deep thinker. It was he who got me reading for the first time in my life – inspirational stuff like *Awaken The Giant Within*. Of all the books he shoved my way the most useful and most influential was *The Psychology of Cricket* by Graham Winter. This was where I started to pick up simple but crucial things like forgetting about the last ball, putting it out of your mind, and concentrating on the next. Belly and I would spend hours, as we drove to games, talking about these aspects of the game. We became close friends, and I was delighted when he was awarded a two-year contract at the end of that first season. He'd put in some good performances for us as an all-rounder, and shown that on his day his left-arm swing bowling was just about unplayable. Belly also got me to take an interest in personal grooming. He was a real snappy dresser, immaculately turned out, and always trying to get me to tidy myself up.

Another guy I got to be friendly with was Roger Twose, a real tough lad who – because he was built like one – was nicknamed

CHAPTER 11 : LIVING A DOUBLE LIFE

Buffalo. He came from Devon and had the west country accent to go with it. An all-rounder, he hustled and bustled and was always into new ideas. He was the first guy I saw writing reminders on his gloves: *Watch The Ball, Play in the V,* and so on. On his cricket bag he had *Supreme Ball Focus,* and one I really liked: *Play the ball not the man.* It may sound frivolous, but these are the basics of the game that you need to keep reminding yourself of, the things that you're inclined to forget once you start worrying about a bowler's reputation, or the state of the game, or your recent failures. Twosey was three or four years older than me and had been on the staff a while. I looked up to him. He was one of those players who really got up the opposition's noses. He was full of himself and could be quite arrogant, but I loved the guy. When Brian Lara arrived in 1994, fresh from having made a world record 375 for the West Indies, he found a note in his locker, 'welcome to the second best left-hander in the world', and we all knew who'd put it there.

As well as my actual mates in the seconds there were one or two senior pros who took me under their wing. Paul Smith – or Worzel Gummidge as we called him – was always laughing and joking, but he was a very caring sort of guy who would always listen to you and help you out in any way he could. At a time in my career when I was getting quite down because it seemed I'd never break through, it was he who took the trouble to call me, arrange to meet, and encourage me to get my head down and keep plugging away. Young players need this sort of help, and it's not easy to know where to find it. The fact is that as an opening bat, for example, the last person you'd turn to is another opener. Why should he be interested in helping you iron out any kinks in your game when you're both competing for the same vacancy? I'm not saying we'd go as far as Geoff Boycott, who famously told another opener that he'd worked out a certain Australian bowler but wouldn't pass on the benefit of his wisdom because 'that's for me to know and you to find out', but we all had an instinct for self-preservation.

One of the biggest shocks to my system at this level was the realisation that my fielding was nowhere near the required standard. As an Asian myself I don't think I can be accused of bias if I say that young Asian kids – then and now – tend to neglect their fielding. They feel that if they bat well and bowl well, and with style and panache, then that's enough. Of course, it isn't. At any level, if you can turn a four into a three by dashing round the boundary and diving full-length, or save runs by cutting off a drive in the covers, you can make a real difference to the other side's total. In one-dayers, of course, 10 runs here or there can be absolutely crucial. So many of these games go down to the wire. You only have to think of how England's Ashes victory in 2005 hinged on a two-run win at Edgbaston to realise that fielding is a vital part of the game. With youngsters who actually grow up in the sub-continent you have to bear in mind the kind of playing surfaces most of them have out there: rock hard, and not really inviting the kind of full-length dive you can execute on England's green and pleasant fields.

My inadequacies in the field were pointed out to me in my first season of second XI cricket. We were playing at home against the Midland Club Conference. I was in the covers, and someone played a fairly innocuous drive in my direction. I bent down, way too casually, to pick it up one-handed – and gave away two runs as the ball bobbled past me. I got a lot of stick for that, not just from the bowler but also from the rest of the guys. It was pointed out to me in no uncertain terms that it wasn't just my lack of concentration, but a basic lack of fitness that was letting me down in the field, making me slow to get to the ball. In addition, I wasn't reading the game as I should, and was unable to anticipate where the ball was likely to be played. After that incident, Neal Abberley gave me hours of extra practice – and another stern talking-to, with the result that I learned to concentrate on every ball and maintain it through every session.

This willingness of the coaches at Warwickshire to work on every aspect of your game reflected their basic professionalism. They even had a guy come over from America, a baseball player, to improve our throwing techniques. The result of all this was that we knew we could throw the ball in better and so put the squeeze on opposing batsmen, turning threes into twos, and twos into singles, and then as the pressure mounted they'd become anxious to move on, and sooner or later would take a risk against the wrong ball or chance a dodgy single. Our throwing became faster and more accurate, and our wicket-keeper, Keith Piper, taught us all to aim for his chest to give him a nice comfortable take over the stumps. Teamwork, that's what it was all about.

Warwickshire's professional approach to the game wasn't restricted to the technical aspects either. Everything about the set-up made you feel good about yourself, and proud of your status. When you showed up

CHAPTER 11 : LIVING A DOUBLE LIFE

pre-season, for example, there would be a big black bin-liner waiting for you with your name on it, full of gear: 10 shirts, several pairs of white trousers, a pile of sweaters, three or four pairs of cricket boots and so on. And in return we were expected to display a similar professionalism. We were told to show up for every training session clean shaven, and well turned out. As far as I was concerned, personal grooming became an important part of how you present yourself to the world. If you want respect, you need to show that you respect yourself. These were the seeds of my later interest in lifestyle training as an accompaniment to cricket training, developing not just the sportsman but the whole individual.

As I settled into my new career as a pro, I realised I was to some extent living a double life. The guys I played with at the county had no idea what it was like in Small Heath, where life was pretty bleak for a lot of the families I'd grown up with. Ours was a decent house, but it was only a three-bed terrace. We had a tiny bath, but no such thing as a shower. My room was maybe 10 feet by 6 with a narrow bed and a couple of basic items of furniture. I did have my own little television there, and loved to lie in bed watching it, but otherwise our living conditions were pretty basic. Out through my window I looked onto a garden which still consisted of a bumpy area of rough grass, a broken-down fence separating us from other similar plots. I could hardly complain about that, since I was responsible for at least one missing board. It was only later, after I'd grown up, that Mum started planting flowers and taking an interest in the garden. When I was younger it wouldn't have been worth it as we kids were always hurtling through on our way to someone else's house, leaping the fences and trampling the soil. To the front of the house, the road was strewn with litter, and as often as not there'd be a burned-out car at the corner, abandoned by joy-riders. Nevertheless, when I came home from a day's practice, I'd still be there in the street some nights, or climbing over the gates into the school playground to join in a game with the same old milk-crates, tennis balls and splintered bats.

Compare all that with the luxury lifestyle I encountered when we were playing away. The first thing was the hotel staff calling you sir, which made me acutely uncomfortable. Here were these men and women, often far older than I was, acting as if I was better than them in some way. That wasn't the way I was brought up, which was to respect your elders. And then to be shown into a lovely room all of your own, with a

CHAPTER 11 : LIVING A DOUBLE LIFE

flashy shower and a deep bath and great thick warm towels. A lot of the guys seemed to take all this for granted. I was totally in awe of it at first.

It was as if I was commuting between two different worlds. At home I still spoke Punjabi, at the cricket ground English. Even my personality seemed to have two sides to it now. At the ground I was one of the boys, joining in the banter, learning to talk like they talked, cracking jokes, trying to be like them. Back at the house I was the person I'd always been, deferential to my Mum, respectful to the elders, very much a member of the community and relishing the spirit we had there. We still referred to Small Heath as 'the ghetto', and took pride in our togetherness, our relative success built on limited resources and hard work. Returning from an away game to the place I'd grown up in, I always felt a sense of relief, and usually a little humility too, much as I enjoyed my trips away.

It was an odd situation I was in, because cricket is a very real and deep passion for most Pakistani people. Many of them were thrilled at my modest success, yet in order to succeed in that world I was having to live this double life and in some ways move away from my roots. Of course, not everyone in 'the ghetto' was thrilled about what I was doing. There were one or two, the sort of negative people you'll find anywhere, who delighted in telling me how badly I was doing – and of course, at this stage I'd never made much money at the game. I would have been better off financially working at Wimbush's, my Dad's old bakery. But I learned to ignore them. I was pursuing a dream, and so far I felt pride in what I'd achieved. My father had always told me that I'd have to work twice as hard in this country to get anywhere in life, and at times I thought that was true in the world of county cricket. There were certainly some tough times ahead.

However, the second XI scene was fun to start with, and exciting. They were a great bunch of lads, and we gelled well together. I started living out of a suitcase, sometimes being away for five days a week. As well as my occasional second XI starts there were games for Smethwick, the under-19s, England Schools and the odd representative game. At one stage that first year I played 44 games in 47 days. I found that what a lot of other cricketers say is true: your body goes onto auto-pilot, even though there are days when you struggle to get out of bed due to the various aches and sprains that stiffen up in the night.

CHAPTER 11 : LIVING A DOUBLE LIFE

I probably looked up to Roger Twose more than anyone else. I studied the way he played, noted the focus in his eyes. Like me, he was a left-hander, and I learned a lot from him. We were in a sense all trying to outdo each other, which for the coaches was cricketing heaven: keen competition for limited places. Some of the guys took it a bit far, though. I remember the day when Jason Ratcliffe, another opening bat, and Piran Holloway almost came to blows when Piran ran his partner out. Piran was a nervy sort of guy who'd undermine your confidence if you took too much notice. You'd be walking out to bat and he'd look at the ground, shake his head and say, 'I wouldn't be surprised if someone got their head knocked off on that track, mate.' He really knew how to cheer you up. 'Tell you what, Waz,' he said one time after an early morning look at the pitch, 'I'm glad it's you opening and not me, it's a definite broken finger job on that wicket.' Anyway, that was Piran. When he ran Jason out there was a bit of verbal that nearly came to blows. Jason wasn't a guy to take any crap from anyone, but really their little bust-up just reflected the anxiety we all felt about taking advantage of every opportunity to show what we could do. The last thing you wanted was some pillock running you out just when you were set, but if your luck was out, what could you do about it?

A lot of players say you make your own luck. They follow the line Bill Shankly, the old Liverpool manager, took when he said, 'Funny isn't it, the harder we work the luckier we get.' You did your best, but you couldn't do anything about luck. You just took what was coming.

I came into second XI cricket feeling confident in my ability. I felt then and I feel now that if I'd managed to get a chance in the first team that first season I would've done well. I feared no one and I played my shots. Unfortunately for me there is a culture in English cricket, as in many other sports, that a player has to 'serve his time'. In Pakistan and India youngsters of 16 and 17 are thrown into state sides. They get the chance to prove themselves before they have developed doubts and insecurities about their game. Hassan Raza and Sachin Tendulkar represented their country at 16. They can't have been the finished article, but being selected gave them the confidence to flourish. Imran Khan spotted a young Waqar Younis while watching a local match on the telly, and Wasim Akram while he was bowling at the Pakistan team in the nets. Inzamam ul Haq was another one unearthed by chance and thrown in at the deep end.

CHAPTER 11 : LIVING A DOUBLE LIFE

Imran had no doubts: he put them into the squad, and they repaid his confidence a hundred times over. People will tell you, 'Ah well, English players take longer to develop.' The question is, could they develop faster if they were given the opportunity?

So I soon started to feel I was drifting in the game, and in a way I have to thank my family for keeping me on the straight and narrow. As soon as I got home my Mum would always want to know how I had got on and would let me talk about my insecurities. She is a deeply religious lady who believes in the power of prayer, and I have to thank her for the faith she instilled in me from a young age. I have always fallen back on that faith in times of adversity, and it has helped me through. It has taught me that things are rarely as bad as they might seem, and that we can always hope for a better tomorrow. I never made an issue of my religion around the other guys I played with, however. I kept it to myself. And I never even thought about fasting during Ramadan while I was playing. It would have been too hard on my body. That's one of the things I like about being retired from the game: I can be a more observant Muslim, and join with my fellow believers in these time-honoured practices. People think that fasting is some sort of ritual punishment of the flesh. Not at all: it instils self-discipline and enables the individual to put other aspects of his life into perspective.

For the moment, then, I was apparently in a rut, playing in the seconds – Magoo cricket, as we called it – and some of my friends and relatives outside the game started to question the time I was spending away from home. Because I wasn't in the limelight they presumed I must be failing. And to tell the truth I started to wonder too. In 1992 I scored almost 1,000 second XI runs at an average of 36.26. Not great, but not bad. In 1993 my average had slipped to the mid-20s, and I had yet again failed to make the breakthrough. The first team were having a desperate season in the Championship; nobody averaged above 40 and the side finished 16th. Luckily, they redeemed themselves with a fantastic performance in the NatWest Trophy final, overhauling Sussex's daunting 321 off the final ball to grab the trophy. But I was more concerned with my own situation. It would take all my resources – application, determination, self-belief, and my faith – to see me through another winter Down Under with the same aim, of at last getting into the first team the following season.

After two enjoyable and successful winters at North Perth, way out on Australia's 'western frontier', I now moved to Albion CC

CHAPTER 11 : LIVING A DOUBLE LIFE

in Melbourne. Belly was out there with me, and at his instigation I did a lot more reading and got myself mentally focussed. I also learned a bit about housekeeping and looking after myself. That was a bit of a culture shock after home, where Mum, in the traditional way, wouldn't let me lift a finger around the house. It was all a part of my ongoing education.

I was now at a critical stage in my career: 23 years old and surely, surely, ready to step up. There was already one cloud on the horizon, however. Before we flew out Warwickshire had made an announcement that had eyes popping all over the cricketing world. Their overseas player next year would be none other than Brian Lara. It was a great coup for the county and, some would argue, for the English game. It would doubtless benefit us all as county batsmen to play alongside such a gifted and accomplished individual, but it was hard not to feel a shiver of fear. What would Lara's arrival do to my chances of getting into the first XI?

Well, he was coming, and I might as well enjoy it. In fact, I looked forward to meeting him, and to seeing him play. I would surely learn from a player who had so recently taken the England attack for 375 runs and set a new world record for an individual score in a Test match. Instead of lamenting his arrival, I set my stall out to play alongside him. I upped my practice hours, staying on after everyone else had gone, getting my mates from home to come and bowl or throw balls at me in the nets – throwing rather than bowling, from 15 yards or so rather than 22 to sharpen up my reflexes. Later that year I would have the privilege of doing that kind of practice with Brian Lara. I was absolutely amazed how just about every ball, 19 out of 20, came back to me so hard and fast, and always off the middle of the bat. We're not talking about half volley balls either: he insisted I hurled the ball in at all sorts of angles and heights, making it as awkward as possible for him to play a controlled shot. But back they came, hard and fast and true.

By the time the new season started I was feeling as sharp as I'd ever been. I went into our first second XI game, a three-dayer against Leicestershire at Grace Road, feeling relaxed and confident. The wicket was a bit green, but I wasn't going to let that worry me. I was going to bat all day. I was going to bat so well that they'd have to pick me and I'd play alongside the world's greatest batsman, Brian Lara. Sometimes you feel like that and get out in the first over, but this day everything went my way. I was seeing the ball early, my timing was perfect, and everything I tried was coming off. By the tea interval I was on 90, and afterwards I passed the 100 mark in the best possible way, sending three consecutive balls to the boundary. At close of play I had 140 not out, and a few days later when I was back at Edgbaston, there was Brian Lara himself, walking over to shake my hand. 'It's Wasim, isn't it? Heard about your hundred. Well played.' Moments like that are special to a young cricketer. I felt like a million dollars.

Like all great players, Brian has the knack of making everything he does look easy. As a guy, I think he suffered during my time at Warwickshire from the immense media and public interest in him. People started to think he was becoming aloof and distant at times. I think he just wanted to keep his mind focussed on the job in hand, scoring runs for his adopted county, and at this he was supremely successful. He's the only guy I've ever seen who could score 100 before lunch and then doss down in the dressing room for a kip. What's often forgotten about his amazing season with the Bears is that he wasn't the county's first-choice overseas player. If Indian batsman Manoj Prabhakar hadn't got himself injured after agreeing to play for us, the world's greatest batsman would probably have spent the summer of 1994 with his feet up in the West Indies.

It's been well documented that Brian didn't get on with our captain, Dermot Reeve. There are things to be said on both sides. Firstly, Dermot isn't the easiest guy to get along with: he's opinionated and he gets under people's skins. But then a captain should have strong opinions, and getting under the opposition's skins is part of the game. If you can wind them up and break their concentration, that's all to the good. Besides Dermot's personality, however, was the fact that Brian clearly regarded him as a pretty average cricketer. When the Bears were playing Leicestershire, the pair of them were fielding at first and second slip and Phil Simmons, the West Indian batsman, was at the crease. Just to gee things up, Dermot said, 'Can you believe that guy plays Test cricket with a technique like that?' Brian wasn't amused. 'That guy's made Test hundreds,' he said. 'What have you ever done?'

Before the season had started I'd been talking with Raja. Raja had sort of drifted in the game after playing for England at under-15 level, and was no longer with the county. He was four or five years older than me, but Amjad, Parvaz and I had all known him well when we were growing up in Small Heath. He was something of a role model and mentor to us younger guys. He'd gone on to university and was now teaching at

CHAPTER 11 : LIVING A DOUBLE LIFE

George Dixon school, not far from where we all grew up. He had many interests, and was thought of as a bit of an operator. He was well connected and had always been a natty dresser: sharp suit, flashy watch, and a fast car to go with it. He had the gift of the gab: we always said he could sell a bucket with a hole in it, so it was no great surprise when he started to operate as a freelance agent – nor when he started to make enemies at Edgbaston, arranging for promising young players to get contracts elsewhere when they hadn't been offered better ones at Warwickshire. But that never got in the way of his love of cricket and his interest in our development. He really wanted us to make the grade. As he saw it, the community needed a few success stories. So he advised me. As an opener, he argued, I was there to set the innings up. Opening was a specialist position. It was the later batsmen who would thrash it around. I should keep my head down, build an innings. Which is what I did. The next three innings yielded 55, 77 and 61, all not out. It set the pattern for the rest of a season in which I continued to score heavily in the various grades of cricket I played, but restrained my natural tendencies, which were to attack.

As to getting into the first team, though, the prospects were looking bleak. Those guys were playing out of their skins. Twosey averaged 55, and Dominic Ostler and Andy Moles were making hay, as were Graeme Welch and Dougie Brown. In all, seven batsmen averaged over 35 that Championship year, and top of the pile was the phenomenal Lara. Not satisfied with smashing the record for an individual Test score, he now set his sights on another. He kicked off the season with a big 100 against Glamorgan, just 11 days after the 375 in Antigua, and proceeded to score 1,167 runs in seven innings before the first week in June was out. Along the way he piled up 501 in a county game against a hapless Durham, breaking Hanif Mohammed's record of 499, which had stood for almost half a century. As a Warwickshire fan I loved it; as a Warwickshire second XI opener, waiting for the step up, it just about broke my heart.

As the season wore on and the first team carried all before them, my fears that I might never get into the side became overshadowed by the thought that I might have to move elsewhere. And then there was my actual ability: was there something wrong with my game, or was I just unfortunate to be at a county blessed with an abundance of talent where everyone was on a hot streak at once? It was a bit like being a top reserve at Manchester United.

CHAPTER 11 : LIVING A DOUBLE LIFE

Any move would be a drop down, but you surely couldn't stay forever. Sometimes I couldn't help looking at other players who had made the transition, and wondering how they managed it. Dominic Ostler, for example, had made his debut early after barely a handful of second XI appearances. He'd deserved it, no question about that, but I felt that I'd deserved a chance too, and I hadn't had one. He'd got his break under Andy Lloyd's captaincy, back in 1990. Lloyd clearly liked Dom's game. I couldn't say the same about Dermot and me. As time went by I was starting to get more frustrated and finally angry. Other players seemed to be getting on, and I was getting stale. Time was passing me by. The worst of it was knowing that other players rated me, but even after four years as a contracted pro I was no nearer than I was in year one. It was all very well for Dermot to come up and say, as he did more than once, 'Keep going, mate; we've got our eye on you, you're in the shake-up,' but in the end I stopped listening. Hoping became too painful. When I saw him coming over for a chat in the nets I switched off. I knew the script by now.

One of the guys I drew closer to was Asif Din. He was a well-established member of the first team, but had found himself shoved further and further down the batting order throughout his career. He will always be best remembered for his innings in the 1993 NatWest final against Sussex when the Bears were chasing that daunting 321. It was his dashing 102 that swung the game in our favour. When he went to the crease he was not alone in presuming that this was his last game for the county. His reward was a further contract and a benefit year in 1994. We often chatted about the significance of that innings. For him it was a case of justice being done. God had helped him through, and his faith had been rewarded. I drew a lot of comfort from that as I watched the first team march to an unprecedented treble: Championship, Sunday League and Benson and Hedges Cup. A few days later I signed another one-year contract, then packed my bags for my now annual visit Down Under.

CHAPTER 12

'I think you're playing'

WHEN I flew home from Melbourne the following spring I was composed, I was focussed, and I was fit. Playing for Albion CC in the Sunshine League wasn't the toughest cricket I'd experienced, but I'd enjoyed my games and I'd worked harder than I'd ever worked in my life. I was up at six, out into the deserted streets of St Albans, and down the road to the running track that circled the local Aussie Rules field. On the way home, I'd enjoy the quiet of the early morning, cooling myself off by running through the sprinklers that watered the lush suburban lawns. It was good to be out and about at that time with the sun just rising. By nine o'clock the temperature would be nudging 30 degrees.

So I was in good heart and in good shape, ready for what really was a make-or-break year. There was no question about that. I was coming up to 24, I'd made my second XI debut five years ago, and I'd watched other players like Michael Bell and Dominic Ostler accelerate past me into the first team, although Belly had succumbed to injury. But at least he'd had his chance, and taken it, grabbing 29 wickets in five games before his back went. Dom had been capped at 19, and was well established. Now it was my turn. It had to be.

I'd watched the first team sweep the board the previous year, and I'm not going to say it didn't hurt like hell that they managed that without me, although they managed without quite a few others too: only 17 players appeared in Championship games that year. I was well aware that it would take something special to break into such a successful team. It's hard not to let envy turn into jealousy in situations like that. Sometimes when I looked at that team I thought of old mates, like Parvaz for example, who'd moved to Worcestershire. Maybe if I'd gone somewhere like that, somewhere where the expectations weren't quite as high, I'd be an established first-team player by now. Maybe I'd set my sights too high. As an opener at Edgbaston I'd been competing with guys like Nick Knight, now a member of the England squad, New Zealander Roger Twose and Jason Ratcliffe. Jason, however, had moved to Surrey over the winter, so if Nick got an England call there had to be an opening for me. There just had to be.

Sometimes, yes, I did start to feel despondent, but no way was I ready to quit.

CHAPTER 12 : 'I THINK YOU'RE PLAYING'

I only had to think of my father, who'd worked so selflessly and never had time to achieve what he wanted to do in life. He'd always told me that it wasn't enough to be good enough: you had to really stand out before people would accept you. Then there was my mother, giving me so much practical support, as well as offering up prayers for me. When I thought about all she'd done, allowing me to pursue my dream despite my father's death, it renewed my determination. It was a determination fuelled at times by anger, anger at always being told you had to 'do your time' in the seconds. How much time did they want, for God's sake? If you were good enough you were old enough. Simple as that. Leave a player waiting too long and insecurity and doubts start to eat away at his self-confidence. It's a vicious circle.

I wasn't alone in my frustration. How many times had I sat out a rainy afternoon at some godforsaken out-ground talking with mates like Graeme Welch about the injustice of it all, and with guys from other counties in similar straits, doomed to eke out their career in the seconds before they lost the will to carry on? But now even Graeme had made it to the firsts, so where did that leave me? Feeling lonely and isolated, among other things. And humiliated. How many times had Dermot Reeve come up and given me a word of encouragement? 'Keep it going, Waz, you'll get there.' Bollocks. In the end it was like you were being patronised.

Worse than that, the whole business was starting to unsettle my mind. I kept casting around to find reasons why they never picked me, but I couldn't. I'd had a good season in the seconds, averaging 40. Everyone told me I was coming on great, over and over until it started to sound like they were bullshitting. Maybe they had convinced themselves my time had gone, and they were scared to tell me. Or were they scared to pick me in case I proved them wrong and made them look stupid? Round and round in my head the arguments raged, to and fro.

I started retreating – into my own head. At home I was short with people. When I went back to Somerville Road after an away trip, all I wanted was to get away from cricket, but people always wanted to ask me questions. How's it going? Why aren't you in the first team yet? What's up, Wasim? Why don't you want to talk? Surely you can talk to your uncle. You haven't seen him since you were little and he's flown all this way.

They meant well, most of them, but it was as much as I could do not to tell them all to

CHAPTER 12 : 'I THINK YOU'RE PLAYING'

sod off and leave me alone. How could they know what it felt like to arrive home at one in the morning when you'd driven all the way from Taunton having dropped two catches and been run out just when you'd dug yourself in for a long innings? How could they know that you needed time alone to get your head straight? Looking back, it can't have been any easier for them than it was for me.

In the end I fought the pain with anger and defiance and directed it at the first-teamers. Right, you bunch of tossers, I'll show you. You can stick together in your little cliques and pick each other game after game, but in the end I'm going to make it impossible for you to ignore me. You had your big year in 1994. 1995 is my year. Just you wait and see.

1995 was to start, as several seasons did, with a warm-up tour to South Africa. This was one of the great advantages of playing for an outfit like Warwickshire: they could afford this sort of thing. As a seasoned second-teamer and a contracted pro I had assumed that I would be going. I'd even talked to the guys about it, and nobody had told me otherwise. Then one morning, during a routine practice session, I was asked to pop into the dressing-room.

You always know when they've got bad news for you. They call you to the dressing-room. I can't remember ever being called to a meeting in there to hear good news. Always bad. If they had good news they'd tell you in the nets or out on the field. No need for privacy then.

As I made my way up the steps to the pavilion, still panting from one of the fielding routines we'd been doing, I couldn't imagine what was on their minds. We were only two days into training. What could have happened? What was on Dermot's mind? When I opened the door, however, it wasn't our captain who greeted me, it was Tim Munton, looking distinctly uncomfortable.

'Hey Tim, what's up?'

'Oh shit, Waz.'

'What? What is it?'

'Dermot was going to tell you but he got called away.'

'Tell me what?'

'They're taking Anurag.'

'Taking him where, mate?'

'To South Africa. Instead of you.'

I was running. Round and round the boundary, circuit after circuit, past the pavilion, past the sightscreens, past that spot where I'd busted in through the fence all those years ago when everything seemed possible and the world was there for the taking. Training had finished and everyone else had gone home, and there I was still

CHAPTER 12 : 'I THINK YOU'RE PLAYING'

pounding round the perimeter as the rain swept in across the empty terraces, waiting for my rage to subside. But it wouldn't. So I kept running. Fuck them all. Dermot Reeve. Anurag too. Yeah sure, he was a decent guy and a real flair player, and later on I'd get to like him, but right now all I could think was, 'What's he ever done for the county?' Okay, he'd scored a lot of runs for England under-19s in the Windies last winter, but so had I when I was playing at that level. Four hundreds in five innings. What had he done for Warwickshire, that's what I wanted to know? Where was he when I was banging out big scores week after week in the seconds? He was at Cambridge, studying law and playing on featherbed wickets at Fenners. Now he was walking into the touring party. And I was running, repeating to myself, 'Have faith. You'll get you what you deserve.' I had to believe it.

Belly felt as aggrieved as I did; he was straight in to support me. It was an outrage, he said; unfair, plain bloody stupid. What were they doing, trying to destroy me? Trev Penney was even more angry. He was ready to fight my corner for me. 'It's a disgrace, mate. I can't believe it. I'll sort the bastards out, right now.' In the end I had to restrain him. It was my battle, not his, and I was the one who had to fight it. Maybe I should've taken a leaf out of Trev's book, after all. But instead of letting the coaching staff have it right in their faces I just dished out more punishment to myself, running and running until the physical pain wiped out the heartache.

The coaches thought it was great, the way I was responding to adversity by knuckling down to it, flogging my way round the ground day after day after everyone had gone home – those who weren't soaking up the South African sun, that is. They didn't think it was so great when they got a call from Raheena to say I'd got home and collapsed, that I was in hospital suffering from exhaustion and severe dehydration.

I was out of action for three weeks, so I never really got much chance to meet up with new coach Phil Neale, who'd arrived that winter to take over from Bob Woolmer. He was an unknown quantity. What would he think of me? Would he want to make his own mind up, or would he just ask Dermot? 'Waz? Yeah, sure. Showed a lot of promise. Never really moved up a gear.' I could almost hear it in my mind, and I wanted to break in and tell them: I never had a chance.

By the time I'd recovered the season was under way and of course I was in the seconds. I got my first game against Northampton. It was at one of our out-grounds, Knowle and

CHAPTER 12 : 'I THINK YOU'RE PLAYING'

Dorridge CC in leafy Solihull. I liked playing there. It was a good quick wicket with an extremely fast outfield, and it was in a beautiful setting – an affluent neighbourhood, big houses, nice trees, the lot. With my illness behind me, I was feeling up for it again. Say what you want about me in those days, but I was resilient, always ready to come back and take some more of whatever was going to be dished out to me.

Once again, Fate wrong-footed me. We hadn't exactly performed brilliantly the first couple of days, and now we found ourselves with a mountain to climb: 330 to win from 80 overs. Phil Neale was supposed to be there the second day but he'd been called away on some sort of committee meeting, so it was my good fortune that he showed up on the final day to see me hit 150 as we polished off the target with overs to spare. I'd seen him sitting at the far end of the ground, chatting to Neal Abberley, and when we came off he was first to congratulate me.

'That was a hell of an innings. Well done, mate.'

'Thanks.'

'Must be in contention to get back in?'

'Yeah right.' As I took I off my pads I glanced up at him. He was frowning.

'What does that mean?'

'I've been in contention for quite a while.'

'So how many first-team games have you had?'

'You want to know?'

I knew I was pushing it, and he was starting to look irritated. 'Why else would I ask you?'

'Let's say it's a nice round number.'

He didn't say anything else. He didn't need to. If he couldn't read the look on my face he had no business being a coach, and he was a very good one. He was a good man-manager too; in fact that was more his forte. He'd captained a successful Worcestershire team when they'd had a line-up that included Graeme Hick, Ian Botham and Graham Dilley. It says something for a guy who never played for England and who captained Lincoln City in the football season that he could do that. They were big personalities, major figures in the international game. But they respected him.

The day after the Northants game I showed up at Edgy as usual, changing at the indoor school with the second-team guys. I'd woken up a little sore after the previous day's effort, and as I prepared for the usual practice routines I took things a bit steady, paying particular attention to my fluid intake.

Just as I was pulling on my whites I saw Asif Din come in through the door and walk

CHAPTER 12 : 'I THINK YOU'RE PLAYING'

across towards me. He was a senior pro by this stage in his career, in and out of the first team and captaining the seconds.

He spoke very quietly, but I remember every word he said. 'Get your things together. Nick Knight's not fit. I think you're playing.'

As I walked across to the first-team dressing-room and took a seat I played the words over and over again in my head. I think you're playing. I think you're playing. I think you're... Why 'think'? Why not 'you're playing'? Had they got someone else in mind? Were they going to re-jig the order at the last minute and make me 12th man?

But there I was getting changed and nobody came to tell me I wasn't in. The TV was droning on in the corner where Twosey and Neil Smith were arguing the toss about who England should be picking against the Windies. Across the other side someone was playing Alanis Morrisette to put them in the mood. One by one the boys came over and wished me luck, and slowly – very slowly – it dawned on me that I really was in the side. Then I looked up and Allan Donald was putting a hand on my shoulder. 'Mate,' he said, 'it's been a long journey for you, but you're here now. Don't let it slip away. This is where you want to be, remember? This is where that long road leads.' That felt good, because Allan was the ultimate pro as far as I was concerned. An Afrikaner, he'd come to Birmingham hardly speaking a word of English and had taken the county game by storm. 'White Lightning' was a team player through and through, a real 110 percenter. You wanted to do well for a guy like that.

We'd won the toss and Dermot had decided to bat. I wouldn't have long to wait. With the line-up we had in those days – and the confidence that comes with success – our game plan was to make a big score, bowl the opposition out twice, and enjoy a day off. As I started to put my gear on according to my usual routine – right pad, left pad, box, thigh guard – I looked around the dressing room. Dermot Reeve was having his back rubbed, Dougie Brown and Gladstone were cracking jokes, others were grabbing a last-minute energy bar or a drink of Gatorade. The place smelled of Ralgex and sweat, with a whiff of deodorant.

I slipped on my helmet and gloves, then picked up my bat and went through a few of my usual drills: ducking a bouncer; driving and cutting; then that same old forward defensive that Pete Bolland had spotted in the playground all those years ago... and then quite suddenly the umpire was at the door in his white coat. 'Gents, we're on our way.' Then I heard the bell, and, as I made

CHAPTER 12 : 'I THINK YOU'RE PLAYING'

for the door with Andy Moles, the words of encouragement.

'Good luck.'

'Your day, Waz.'

'C'mon, fellas, get us off to a good start now.'

'Be there at lunch, boys.'

We trotted down the steps, and as we made our way through the gate and onto the field there were a couple of shouts, 'Come on you Bears' and a ripple of 'good lucks' before I heard my name announced over the loudspeakers. 'Wasim Khan.' It seemed to hang in the still air, and for a brief moment I felt a sadness that my Dad couldn't be there to witness the moment. I said a silent prayer, puffed out my chest, held my head up high and approached the wicket. It was a hazy sort of morning, with a nice warm day in prospect. There were a couple of thousand in the ground, pretty good for a county game. As I marked out my guard I looked around and saw England's Alec Stewart at first slip and Graham Thorpe at second, with ex-England bowler Tony Pigott pacing out his run. Well, I thought, these are the guys you wanted to test yourself against. Better get used to it.

Pigott's first ball was a little short, outside off stump, and an easy one to steer down between third slip and gully. This felt like fun. Andy Moles was down the wicket as the ball crossed the boundary. 'First of many, mate. Now focus again and watch the next one.' As he walked away I heard someone in the slips say, 'Just *nick* the next one to me, mate; I'll be ready. Then we'll have your fat friend.' Andy turned and grinned. He was short and round, and loved his food. When it came to taking the mickey he could dish it out with the best of them. 'Piss off,' he said. I didn't even look around. No way. Maybe when I had 100 on the board.

It wasn't a great innings, in fact a bit of a disappointment because I managed to run my partner out just when he was starting to get set. I punched a shortish one outside off stump and set off for a quick run. Darren Bicknell picked up and scored a direct hit from mid-wicket, with Andy a mile out of his ground. As he trudged past me, a rich Black Country voice boomed across from the terracing: 'Hey, Wasim mate, next time leave a cake out for him – that'll get the bugger moving.' All I could do was apologise – it was my own stupid fault – and all Andy could do was tell me to forget about it. 'Go on and get a ton, mate.'

I didn't set the world ablaze that first game. In the first innings I scored 19 before dragging one onto my stumps, and in the second 25. I wondered what the selectors

CHAPTER 12 : 'I THINK YOU'RE PLAYING'

would think. Not a lot, it seemed. At lunchtime after that first knock I had a chat with Dermot, which hardly set my mind at ease. He told me that when Phil Neale had mentioned my name as a replacement for Nick Knight a member of the selection panel had been dead against it. My time had passed, he reckoned, and they should be looking to the future. But Phil had dug his heels in and had his way. All afternoon as the innings progressed I sat there wondering what the hell Dermot had hoped to achieve, telling me that. Was he playing a subtle psychological game, trying to gee me up? Or was that too generous an assessment? I can think of one or two in the team who would've come to the conclusion that he was just being a complete arsehole. If his intention was to motivate me, it was a strange way of going about it: he could have undermined whatever self-confidence I had left.

As it was, I might not have made a huge hit, but I hadn't failed. The jury was still out, and I'd surely get a second chance. When I got home the night after my first innings, however, it was as though I'd just scored a match-saving 100. It was like a party with friends, family and neighbours all crowding into the house to congratulate me, Mum telling me how she'd been checking my progress on Teletext, and loads of mates phoning to ask why I hadn't told them. When I said that I didn't know I was playing until 10 o'clock that morning they couldn't believe it. Next time, they said, tell us. We'll come and support you. Did that pile the pressure on? No, it felt good. These were my people. They believed in me. Somebody had to.

By the next week I was able to tell them what they wanted to hear: I was in the team to play Lancashire at Old Trafford. This was the ultimate test. Seven internationals including the likes of Atherton and Fairbrother, plus Peter Martin and Glenn Chappie, and of course, my hero, the great Wasim Akram.

I was 13 years old when I first heard his name mentioned. He was playing for Pakistan against New Zealand Down Under. He was just 19 – another example of a young guy being given his head. He hit the headlines big time when he bagged match figures of 10 for 128 in only his second appearance. Later that year, he was up against the mighty Windies, bowling alongside Imran Khan and Abdul Qadir. How's that for a three-man attack? He blew them away: 6 for 91. Now he was taking on the scrawny kid from Somerville Road, the one they still called Buzz. I had three full days

CHAPTER 12 : 'I THINK YOU'RE PLAYING'

to prepare, so I called Raja and got him to come over and feed the bowling machine. And of course advise me. He always had an angle.

I drove up to Manchester with Dermot in his club-sponsored Peugeot 406. He sat in the passenger seat and talked. He was surprisingly open that way. One minute he was talking tactics and cricket theories, the next it was himself and his career. He seemed to be making it clear that he was like the rest of us, insecure, needing to be liked, one of the guys and so on... and then it was back to how I should deal with Akram's away swing. Actually, I'd thought about that a fair bit already, although the most useful advice was to come my way a little later – from an unexpected source.

Despite a reasonable start against Surrey, the pressure was on me now. I needed to perform. In your first game anything can happen. Remember Graham Gooch, starting off his England career with a pair? You shrug your shoulders: cricket's like that. One slip and the bowler's waving you goodbye. If I failed here, however, doubts would set in. But I felt good; I felt alive again; I felt like I was 19 once more. It was all going to be okay. I knew it.

Dermot lost the toss, and Atherton put us in on a cold morning in front of 1,500 spectators. My first ball from Wasim Akram was a bouncer. I couldn't get out of the way in time, it hit my shoulder and flew over wicketkeeper Warren Hegg for four. As my boyhood hero came down the pitch he nodded his head. 'Right, china, that's my loosener, now let's see what you're about.' I looked round at the slip cordon. Atherton with a wry smile on his face, Fairbrother looking at his nails, Crawley giving me the hard stare. This was the business alright – taking on top guys. So let's see what I'm about, shall we?

As Wasim Akram shifted through the gears I survived the first over, even glancing one down to fine leg for a single – and giving Andy Moles the privilege of facing Pakistan's finest. We settled in well that morning, and by lunch had chiselled out 65 valuable runs. I was 38 not out. Neil Fairbrother jogged by me on his way to the pavilion. 'Played, young man,' he said. That felt good. No bullshit, just an honest appreciation from an established pro. As I nibbled at a bit of salad and got stuck into the fluids, my mate Masood from Small Heath called on the mobile. 'Great start, Waz mate. I'm on my way over with a couple of the lads. See you at close of play.'

That was one of the great wasted journeys of all time. Right after the break I got a

CHAPTER 12 : 'I THINK YOU'RE PLAYING'

classic yorker from my hero and was out without adding to my score.

So far so good, though, and the second innings went even better. It needed to: we were 148 behind. As Andy and I inched our way towards a century stand, I reached my first 50 with a square-cut off Akram. In my mind I dedicated it to my Mum, knowing that she'd be at home, doing the ironing or writing to her relatives back home, but glued to the Teletext. I was still there at tea, full of it. 'Andy,' I said, as we sat in the dressing-room cooling off, 'I'm really gonna go for it now mate. You know – the old pull-shot, maybe go down the wicket, that kind of thing. Show these guys what's what.'

I'd reckoned without Akram being equally determined to prove a point. He sent down one bouncer after another and I couldn't do a thing about it. In an hour and three quarters I smashed... precisely 18 runs, and Moler didn't do much better. But it didn't matter. Here I was, holding my own against the world's best. It was a good feeling, and even when I left one from spinner Gary Keedy and was lbw for 78 just 10 minutes before the close, it didn't seem like the end of the world.

That night I went out for a meal with Gladstone Small and Allan Donald at the Four Seasons Hotel. When we walked in, people turned their heads, nodded and smiled. The head waiter greeted them by name and showed us to a nice table by the window. One or two diners came across and asked them for their autographs – for their sons, of course. I wasn't included in any of this. They had no idea who I was. But I had: I was a young cricketer whose star was in the ascendant. And I loved very minute of it.

Next morning when we were warming up, Wasim Akram came down from the balcony and asked if he could have a word with me. I guess it shows just how good I was feeling that I nearly said, Sorry mate – I'm too busy! As an opening bat you don't usually get your opponents' top bowler wanting to talk to you about your technique – unless they're storming down the pitch to tell you you're a useless frigging plonker, but I was a fellow Pakistani, and in Wasim's eyes we were on the same side. 'You can play,' he said. 'No doubt about that. But you need to watch your stance. It's too open. The top bowlers are gonna spot that and exploit it.' Then he gave me his private number and said that if I ever wanted to call him for advice I'd be welcome. When the game was over and I got back to Small Heath there was another impromptu party at the house, with all sorts of people coming by, even the ones like Aftab who'd told me I was wasting my time

CHAPTER 12 : 'I THINK YOU'RE PLAYING'

chasing success as a cricketer. The funny thing was, most of them were interested in one thing only. What's it like facing Wasim Akram, man? What's his secret? Is he really as fast as he looks?

I faced another Pakistani bowler in the next game: Somerset leg-spinner Mushtaq Ahmed. He didn't bother me: I just kept going down the pitch to counter the spin, and that really pissed him off. We were chasing – well, inching towards – a huge Somerset total, 495, and I was nearing the 50 mark when he walked up to me between overs. 'Listen, Waz, let's do a deal. You get on the back foot and I'll call the hounds off, okay?' I laughed. He had four men round the bat and was really piling on the pressure. 'I'll think about it,' I said. And I did – before deciding that I would carry on the way I was and get right up his nose. I'd reached 89 when I was out lbw to seamer Jeremy Hallett.

How good could it get? I was part of the team now, and part of the dressing-room too. The regular members of the team, guys who'd seemed like a clique, a conspiracy, a few weeks ago, treated me like I'd always been there. They even played practical jokes on me, a sure sign that I belonged. Pulling on my socks before a practice session one morning I put my foot straight through the toe end and toppled forwards as the place erupted in laughter. The phantom snipper had been at work. Next up was Sussex, and another roll of the dice. Nick Knight was fit once more so it was back to the seconds. It was a jolt, but I could take it now. I'd had my chance and I'd grabbed it with both hands. There would be more. I knew there would. There was no stopping me now.

CHAPTER 13

Double winner

BACK in the seconds I was far more relaxed than I had been in an age. I'd done well at the higher level and there would be more chances. My batting was fluent and productive and I ran up four more 100s before being called back into the fold. I felt at ease with the guys now. I roomed with Belly, who was also a regular in the team at this time, and young Ashley Giles was also coming to the party. He'd started out as a seam bowler until back problems forced him to try spinning it. Some people – players and pundits – were surprised when he came good so dramatically against South Africa and Australia in recent Test series, but looking back I remember how he, like Nick Knight, always had a different look in his eyes when it was time to get down to serious work. They both had a real ability to apply themselves. Once more it was a case of working harder and getting luckier. Ash had another thing going for him: great family support. Wherever we played – even in the seconds – half his tribe would be there to applaud him: aunts, cousins, sisters, you name it. We used to call them the Addams family and would whistle the theme tune to the TV series whenever they showed up. I got on well with Ash. We used to travel to away games together in my car until he got his own transport – or was it that he could no longer stand my Elton John cassettes?

As a new member of the team, you expect to be a bit of a dogsbody. When the captain wants a short leg fielder, for example, that's your job. It's not a position that many people will volunteer for – although when your main strike bowlers include Allan Donald and Gladstone Small you're fairly safe: they could always be relied on to maintain a good line, and didn't send too many deliveries down the leg side. But it didn't always work out that way. Matthew Fleming of Kent, for example, liked to get after Neil Smith's off-breaks, and in one match peppered the back of my legs and left me hobbling for days afterwards. At least that gave me an excuse not to field there next time out – although the other players always managed to concoct a dodgy hamstring or a back problem so that they too could stay out of harm's way.

Our new coach Phil Neale worked hard on my fielding – even though my main concern was how far I could retreat as the bowler came in. I found that as I grew in confidence

CHAPTER 13 : DOUBLE WINNER

being a close fielder went well with being an opener, although I was happier at silly point. There you at least had a chance to see the batsman winding up for a square drive or something. But in general it strengthened my ability to concentrate for long periods. It was a little like being a wicketkeeper. You had to watch every ball, and you had to react fast. I snapped up 15 catches there that season, including a crucial one at Ilford, where I got England's Graham Gooch off Donald's bowling, for nought.

As the season progressed towards its climax, I was buzzing. Every game was like a final for me – and for the team. When we played Worcestershire I had the pleasure of facing an attack which included Paul Thomas and Parvaz, thus reuniting three members of our under-13 team from 12 years ago. I think they must have envied me, being in such a great side. We were top of the Championship, and by mid-August had reached the semi-final of the NatWest Trophy. I was top of the averages with 49, although I was still waiting for that elusive first 100. Along the way Phil Neale got together with the county committee and insisted on a wage increase for me. Could it get better than this? I really started to feel a part of what was going on now, joining in the dressing-room banter. I was coming out of my shell. Before long Ashley Giles was asking me to do my Dennis Amiss and Dermot Reeve impressions. One of my favourites was Neal Abberley, with his Brummy way of saying 'hold'. 'Waz, mate, go and get *holt* of Ash and travel up with him.' I even answered Dermot back when he told me to fetch him a cup of tea. 'What, come on Derm, have you lost your legs? I'm busy.'

Dermot was one of those guys you needed to stand up to. On the field, however, I appreciated his value as a leader, and a winder-up of opposing batsmen. Between deliveries he'd clap his hands and shout things like 'Come on, boys, let's have a big team smile' or 'Okay, now let's have some fun in the sun!' And of course he loved to put the fear of God into tail-enders. 'Look,' he'd say, 'I wouldn't hang around if I were you. Otherwise I might have to get Allan Donald back on – and he won't be happy. He was thinking he could put his feet up. Nasty guy when his nose is put out of joint.'

One of his best tricks I first saw in a game against Leicester. A new batsman came to the crease, some young guy we'd never seen before. Dermot walked over and asked him his name. The guy said it was Nigel, and Dermot spent the next few overs calling him by every other name he could think of. Nicely, Dave. Good shot, Tim. Oh, well left,

CHAPTER 13 : DOUBLE WINNER

Bobby. Eventually the young lad turned round, clearly flustered, and said, 'Look, it's Nigel, okay?' – and was out two balls later.

When Dermot had nothing to say, someone like Andy Moles would start a slow handclap as the bowler ran in, and we'd all join him. It can't have been much fun for the batsman, but it wasn't meant to be. We took every game deadly seriously, and expected to win. We were all involved, every ball. Some of our opponents hated us for the way we tried to get on top of them, and here I saw the essential difference between most English sides and the average Australian, for example. In England, self-confidence is quickly put down as arrogance. Over there it's expected that you'll have self-belief. It's seen as wholly positive. You aren't put down for being 'above yourself. As to banter, Dermot had strict rules about that. You simply didn't take the mickey out of another player on account of his form or technique. Players from opposing counties, sure, that was fair game, but among ourselves it was restricted to making fun of a guy's dress sense, that kind of thing. Trevor Penney, for example, had come out from Zimbabwe with a real seventies-style haircut which he refused to alter. Worse than that was his wardrobe: he always dressed as if he was off for a game of golf. Then there were the guys who thought they were God's gift to women. Roger Twose had some of the corniest chat-up lines I've ever heard – apart from Dermot, that is. He was also renowned for having the deepest pockets, and the lads used to try anything to get him to buy his round. In the end someone decided to embarrass him in public. All it took was a little planning, getting someone to distract him for a few minutes in the dressing-room one day at close of play. That evening we all met up in TGI Friday on the Hagley Road. Someone got a round of drinks in, and Twosey soon found himself sitting next to a gorgeous young woman who seemed totally smitten by him. She was deep in conversation with him when Trev Penney leaned across and said, 'Say, Rog, why don't you – you know, buy the young lady a drink, eh?'

'Oh, yeah, sure,' Roger said, pulling out his wallet and trying to open it, nice and casually. But it wouldn't open. Trev had stitched it shut.

And so to Southampton, and that maiden ton. The night before the game I remember chatting with Twosey and Dom Ostler. Roger told us he wouldn't be coming back from New Zealand next year, since he had now qualified to play for their national team and saw a future for himself over there. We

CHAPTER 13 : DOUBLE WINNER

discussed the game ahead. I was aware that we only had five to play, the Championship was at stake, and I still had a personal target to reach. In the morning the pitch looked a perfect batting strip. Unfortunately Hampshire won the toss and batted, but our bowlers put on a superb display and had them all out by about five o'clock. When we went in I lost Roger, then Dom, but I saw out the day on 20 not out, along with nightwatchman Keith Piper.

That night I had a strange dream: I was sitting under a cold shower with all my gear on. What could that mean? I had no idea, but I decided it had to be a good omen. Over breakfast I said to Molesy, 'Mate, I feel good today.' He told me to make sure I concentrated. There were plenty of runs to be had on that track, and we didn't want to miss out.

At stumps, after I'd reached the elusive three-figure target, put on over 200 with Trev Penney and watched Keith Piper get himself out on 99, some of the other lads arrived at Southampton. Asif, Gladstone, Paul Smith and Belly were due to play in the Sunday League fixture that was slotted into the Championship game. They all greeted me with congratulatory hugs, especially Asif. It was a special moment. Even so, I felt a little let down to think that here was the gang assembling for a one-dayer, which I would be missing out on. It has been one regret about my career that I never really developed a game plan for the shortened form, and consequently didn't play very often. Dermot and Bob Woolmer were big fans of all-rounders so the choice was normally between Welchy, Dougie Brown and Paul Smith. It might have been different, but no one ever really sat down with me and talked me through a strategy I could adopt. When I did get a game it was the odd one here and there and I never really felt sure what was required of me. I tended to think I had to score at four an over right from the start, whereas even in a 50-over game you have to give yourself a little time to play yourself in. But then when you did try to ease yourself into the game you could get slagged off anyway. I remember playing a League game against Surrey and leaving a ball outside the off stump. It was only the seventh over, but I was later tackled by my partner. Why had I left it? Why not have a crack? Once again, it was that uncertainty: if I got out, would I make the team next time around? So it was safety first, which wasn't what the team needed.

One-dayers can be hellishly tense affairs, and of course so much can hinge on a single error. Against Kent in a quarter-

CHAPTER 13 : DOUBLE WINNER

final in 1995 I came onto the field, as I often had to, as 12th man. Knighty had been concussed and Trev Penney had his nose broken when the two collided, both going for the same ball. The outcome was in the balance, with Steve Marsh smashing the ball around the ground. We were in desperate need of a wicket when Marshy swung at one. I was fielding on the mid-wicket boundary in front of a packed stand and the ball came right at me, from a great height. I suppose I panicked. I remember standing there thinking, shit, do I take it reverse hands or normal? As ever, indecision was fatal. Before I could make my mind up the ball was through my fingers and over the rope for a six. There was a huge collective gasp from the crowd, but that day fortune smiled on me: Marsh was out in the next over.

By and large at Warwickshire, if a catch went down everyone would get behind you rather than start criticising. The object was to get your confidence up so that you'd pocket the next one. In some teams you'll hear them all go quiet when one gets spilled. That doesn't do anyone any good. I knew I needed to work on my fielding, and I was lucky at Warwickshire, having a guy like Trevor Penney in the squad. He was one of the best fielders in the world. People have compared him to South Africa's Jonty Rhodes, and that's good company to be in. In fact, I would say that Trev had the stronger arm of the two. He has recently become assistant coach for Sri Lanka.

Phil Neale loved his fielding drills, and although they could be fun they were exhausting. He'd have us running round picking a ball off each of 15 or 20 cones and hurling them into him over the stumps. Five minutes of that and you felt like you'd been working out for a week.

Life at the county was great now. I was part of what was happening, part of a winning side. At home, on the other hand, things were getting a little fraught. Basically, my family wanted what all families in our community wanted of their sons: for me to get married and settle down, which was the last thing on my mind at that age. It was my Mum most of all. From her point of view I had a steady job, and that took care of one thing. Now all it needed was a nice wife and life would be perfect for her only son. Quite a lot of my mates had got married young – Amjad, Akhlaq and a few of the others – but I wanted to continue travelling, seeing the world and having a good time with no ties. I knew that some of those guys were secretly envious of what I had, but my Mum kept coming up with

CHAPTER 13 : DOUBLE WINNER

candidates for marriage – and I turned them all down flat. I suppose it must have hurt her at times, but I wasn't wishing to be disrespectful, just to have a say in my own destiny.

Now that I was doing so well, people in the neighbourhood were taking more notice of me. Perhaps they gave me a little more respect. After all, I was in the papers and occasionally popped up on TV. I was still aware of being a bit of a trail-blazer at this stage. I was the one who had broken through. But I didn't want to be some kind of iconic hero, just to show people that it could be done. To this day I see Asian kids struggling to come to terms with the setbacks life throws at them, and I wonder whether they find it harder because they have grown up in a sheltered and nurturing community and don't have to experience the knocks you get in the wider world. It's great to have the sort of support you get from the extended family and neighbours, but it can be a double-edged thing.

After the triumph of my 181 against Hants, it was back to earth with a bump. For the NatWest semi-final at Glamorgan I was dropped, although I travelled down to South Wales with the squad. There was nothing personal in the decision: the needs of the team came first, simple as that.

As it happened, the match itself was a bit of a non-event. In front of a packed Sofia Gardens we bowled the Welsh team out for 80-odd and were packing our bags for home by 4.30pm. Before we wrapped it up, however, we'd seen a rare side to cricket when the crowd, rowdy and abusive and full of alcohol, dished out some ugly abuse to Dominic Ostler, right in front of the pavilion. They told him they were going to 'do' his missus, and then changed tack, calling him a blonde poof. That would have been funny if it hadn't been so threatening, since we used to call him that all the time ourselves. Later, when we were on the balcony celebrating our win, a bottle looped out of the crowd and smashed against the wall right between Andy Moles and me. We dived inside, and left it to our unofficial minder to sort it out. Derek Darby, better known as Rocky, was a massive Warwickshire fan, and had a massive physique to match his enthusiasm. Hence the name: he was a dead ringer for Sly Stallone. He was no hired thug: he had a very successful pine furniture business, but he loved his cricket, came to all the games, and had the bear and ragged staff tattooed on his chest. When the trouble broke out that afternoon he waded into the crowd, grabbed the culprit, pinned his arms to his sides and held onto him until

CHAPTER 13 : DOUBLE WINNER

the police arrived. Even then it wasn't all over. A Glamorgan supporter launched a verbal assault on Allan Donald, calling him South African scum, and a racist. By the time we were ready to leave, we had a police escort to see us on our way in safety.

We were now approaching the climax of another great year. We were out in front in the Championship, but only one win ahead of Middlesex, who had been snapping at our heels all summer. In the last week we had a crucial game against Gloucestershire. Hoping to get into the side for the NatWest final, I was desperate to play, and to get a decent score. To start with things went my way. Nick Knight was struggling with a broken finger, I retained my place, and top-scored with 69 against a good spell by the right-arm fast-medium bowler Javagal Srinath. We got the victory we needed on the final day, and all our thoughts turned to Lords.

For me, just being there with such a great team was a dream come true. We stayed at the Hilton, right opposite the ground, and found the place buzzing with committee men, supporters and players' families. In the evening Knighty and I went out for a meal. I always got on well with him and found him very supportive, even at times like this when we were competing for the same place. He told me that night that he would've had me in the team all summer if it had been up to him. If that was pleasing, what he said when we went back to our rooms really got my pulse racing. He reckoned his finger still wasn't right, and I should be prepared. My heart was pumping when I went to bed, and I fought the urge to pray that his injury didn't get better. There was no way I was going to get off to sleep. Rather than try, I lay there fantasising about the next day, about walking out in front of a capacity crowd, taking my guard, and then rattling up a match-winning 100.

I was halfway through my breakfast when Phil Neale came over. 'Be ready, Waz. Nick's having a fitness test and if he doesn't make it you'll open, mate.' I was almost in a trance as we walked over to the ground, shoving our way between supporters who thumped us on the back and wished us good luck. I'd played at Lord's a few times, but never with a crowd like we were going to see this time – a full house of 30,000. We were due to take the field a few minutes before 11am. At 10.15 I saw Phil walk over towards me. I hardly dared wonder what he was going to say.

'Waz, sorry mate. Knighty's not 100 percent but he wants to play, so he's in.'

Oddly, I got over the disappointment quite quickly. Maybe I'd known all along it was too much to hope for. I went up on the

CHAPTER 13 : DOUBLE WINNER

balcony to watch the crowd gather, and had a few minutes flipping through the papers. I wasn't concentrating at all, just trying to take my mind off what had happened. Then I saw a piece in the *Telegraph* by Nick Cook, the former Northants and England player: who would he pick for the England 'A' tour next winter? I was gobsmacked to see my name there. Would it happen? Was this how the fairytale season would end?

I'd just put the paper down when Phil came up to tell me I was the official 12th man, so I would have plenty to occupy me. Poor Ashley wasn't even in the 12, despite having played a big part in getting us to the final. With the wicket looking green, it was decided to play Michael Bell instead. Actually, Ash would probably have preferred being out of it altogether rather than doing 12th man duties. At Lord's it's a lousy job, trailing up and down those steps from the pavilion every time someone on the field wants a glove, a new bat, a drink, a cloth to wipe a wet ball, a packet of chewing-gum, or maybe the result of the 3.30 at Haydock Park. You have to watch every ball, and constantly be on the look-out for a signal from any one of your teammates scattered around the field. As well as all the fetching and carrying, you're expected to be a glorified head waiter, making sure everyone's lunch is just the way they like it. Some want it in the dining-room, others in the relative calm of the dressing-room so that they don't lose concentration. Then there are the baths to run. Sometimes you're the players' nursemaid too. I once had to fetch Paul Smith's waashing from the local laundrette, and on another occasion had to dash across Birmingham in the rush-hour to collect Belly's car from the Peugeot dealer. No, Ash was well out of it. He could put his feet up and enjoy the game from the balcony.

Northants batted first under grey skies, but had hardly got going when rain stopped play. It came on pretty heavily, and by 4.30pm play was abandoned, a bitter disappointment for the supporters who'd travelled down just for the day. For those who'd booked into hotels in London, however, it was just an extension to the party. Our bar and foyer was heaving with them, as well as wives, girlfriends and children. I managed to call home and heard from Mum that the phone had been ringing all morning with people wanting to know whether I'd made the starting line-up. She was her usual philosophical self. Yes it was disappointing, she said, but it was probably all for a good reason.

CHAPTER 13 : DOUBLE WINNER

Next day the sun shone. Northants got up to 200 on a slow wicket. Run-scoring wasn't easy for them and wasn't going to be easy for us either. But thanks to fighting innings by Dermot Reeve and Roger Twose we closed in on their total in the penultimate over. When Dermot carved the ball through cover for four, the place erupted, and when we all made it to the dressing-room it was pandemonium. The whole team, plus the seconds, the committee, the coaching staff, celebrities like Frank Skinner, violinist Nigel Kennedy – there were all sorts of people in there milling around, hugging each other, drinking champagne. In fact, Phil Neale was held down while one of the lads literally poured the stuff down his throat. Then we had to make our way up onto the balcony for the official presentation. As a great swathe of Warwickshire supporters swarmed around below us David Gower presented us with our medals. I briefly thought back to that time, only 10 or 12 years previously, when I'd carried his bags for him after breaking in through the fence at Edgbaston. I felt awkward about the presentation. Ashley, who had played in most of the previous rounds, should've been up there instead of me – although if I'd known then the way his career would pan out I wouldn't have lost any sleep over nicking a medal from under his nose. He had plenty more good times ahead of him.

The celebrations carried on back at the hotel, but one by one we left the revellers to it and made our way back to Brum, where we partied the night away at the White Swan in Harbourne – nice and handy for Dougie, Ashley, AD and a few of the lads who lived nearby. By 11 o'clock they were all legless and still playing drinking games. Being a non-drinker, I still found it amazing how quickly people changed. I think Dom Ostler was the only other guy who steered clear of the booze. Allan Donald seemed to have the biggest capacity. He drank the way he trained: very hard indeed.

After a victory like that, and the celebrations, your natural tendency is to want to take it easy, but we had work to do. There was one more county championship game against Kent at Canterbury, and we needed a result to clinch the Championship. We had a day's rest, a good work-out at the nets, and then awaited the naming of the squad. I was delighted to hear that both Ash and I were in. I roomed with Ash on this trip. We shared a feeling that this was not only the team's year but ours too. The other guys had done it all before, last season, but this was new to us, as it would be for Allan Donald, who had stepped aside as overseas

CHAPTER 13 : DOUBLE WINNER

player the previous year to make way for Brian Lara. We wanted first of all to make the dream a reality, and then to savour every moment.

At the team talk we stressed the importance of getting a good start. No pressure for the openers, then. But it went like a dream, Nick and I putting on 120 for the first wicket. After one of those stupid mix-ups that happen from time to time I was run out on 51, but Nick went on to get 100, which was, oddly, his first of the season for us. He'd had a strange sort of year, batting consistently well but getting out in the 80s and 90s time after time, so he needed this. Twosey, playing his last game for us, also notched a ton as we piled up the runs and left ourselves almost three days to bowl the opposition out twice. We knocked them over cheaply, enforced the follow-on and as the third day drew to a close we had them nine down. So there we were at the end of a long hard season with Allan Donald steaming in to bowl at Min Patel. AD pulled out a beauty, nicked the outside edge and the ball flew towards Neil Smith at slip. He pouched it safely, AD sank to his knees with his arms raised, and we were champions again.

Within an hour or so we were celebrating in Canterbury, crowding into some local club or other and dancing to the theme from

Hawaii Five-O, which just happened to be playing as we trooped in. There were laughs, there were cheers, there was the clinking of glasses, and the occasional whoop as one of us realised, again, just what we'd achieved. I remember standing there watching Trev Penney as he boogied on down, seventies-style. I was just taking it all in and wondering where I would go from here. I knew how I'd got here all right – by sheer hard work and determination. I'd earned my moment in the sun. It was especially sweet when I thought how unlikely it had all seemed at the start of the season, when I was lying in that hospital bed, but here I was, a regular in a Championship-winning side, scorer of 850 runs in 12 games and averaging 46. I was even 27th in the national averages, edging a certain Graeme Hick into 28th place. For a long time friends and teammates had tried to tell me that things could turn around, but there had been times when I had really started to doubt my own ability. Now I had two medals jangling in my pocket. I felt untouchable, as a man and as a cricketer. I couldn't help thinking about some of the great names of recent times who'd never got within sniffing distance of a Championship. Ian Botham and Viv Richards, for a start. And here I was, top of the tree in my first year. The sky was surely the limit.

CHAPTER 13 : DOUBLE WINNER

Back home there were further celebrations. People were in and out of the house day and night; the phone was constantly ringing; the postman brought congratulatory cards and letters from home and from relatives in Pakistan. I was hearing from people I'd not seen in years, all wanting to tell me they knew – just knew – I'd make it one day. Yes, I said, of course you did.

CHAPTER 14

Swings and roundabouts

UPS AND downs. There's no escaping them. Two weeks later, still on a high, I was asked to play a benefit game for one of the boys, representing my local league against a Worcestershire side. I'd no sooner got to the ground than I had a call from a close friend. Parvaz, Parvaz Mirza, my old mate who'd played with me on the streets of Small Heath, come through the ranks with me at Warwickshire and moved across to New Road, was dead.

This was a shocker. Parvaz and I had travelled the same road through good times and bad. He'd climbed over the fence with me into Andrews, dodging the skinheads; he'd helped me find a way into Edgbaston and stood there with me collecting the five pences from the other kids. He was one of the few guys I knew on the county circuit who really understood what it was like to be in the situations I sometimes found myself in – caught between the gloss of the professional scene and the raw reality of my inner – city home, struggling to make the grade when so many people were saying it

CHAPTER 14 : SWINGS AND ROUNDABOUTS

was never going to happen. Like me, he had seen things turn around, and like me he had just had a great year with his new county. He was a regular in the Worcestershire one-day side and according to Duncan Fearnley and Tom Graveney, speaking on the local TV news that night, was ready to establish himself in the four-day setup. He had just been awarded a two-year contract by the county.

Poor Parvaz. His family were devastated. He left behind a mother, two sisters and two brothers, one of whom, Manir, would later follow in his footsteps and become a pro with Worcestershire. Parvaz had been diagnosed with an irregular heartbeat when he was a kid, but was sure he'd outgrown any problems. He never mentioned it. Now he'd been struck down by a heart attack, at home. Who ever heard of a professional sportsman dying that way? His death affected so many of us. We were all in shock. From the soaring elation of the Championship win my mood plummeted. I became depressed and withdrawn as I struggled to understand why this might have happened. With my family I visited Parvaz's mum daily, trying to comfort and console her. It was the best we could do, remembering what it was like when we saw my Dad taken away so suddenly and how people had rallied round. Sometimes just offering your presence feels so inadequate. It's all you can do, and you have to do it. But I was so devastated I felt wretched that I had nothing else to offer in the way of consolation. In the end it was heartening to see that Worcestershire were in touch with the family, wanting to know how they could help. And it was touching to see all Parvaz's teammates showing up at the mosque for the funeral, a little row of white faces standing behind two or three hundred Muslims as they knelt and prayed for the soul of a lovely young man.

Before this tragic turn of events I had been looking forward to spending my first winter at home for several years. Among the things I wanted to do was to take my Level 1 coaching course. I didn't have a particular desire at that time to become a coach, and I certainly didn't give any thought to life after cricket – that was way too far ahead, almost unimaginable; I'd only just started – but I knew that I wanted to think about ways to put something back into the community I came from, to help other youngsters find some direction in their lives. And, let's be honest, coaching is a great excuse for playing about with a bat and ball, staying close to the physical reality of the great game. I'd coached regularly on my trips Down Under – mostly with junior sides at

CHAPTER 14 : SWINGS AND ROUNDABOUTS

the clubs I was attached to – and enjoyed the experience, even though at North Perth one year I had an under-14 side with five Brads in it.

I was also starting to worry about the younger kids in my own neighbourhood. The next generation on the streets around Small Heath were now exclusively Asian. It seemed to me that they were looking less optimistic than we had been, less cheerful, less motivated to do the things we did. I got the impression that they would play cricket, but that they wanted all the gear to be there for them. Growing up in ever more consumerist times, they seemed to think playing with a home – made bat and a tennis ball would be demeaning. Some of them too were heading for trouble. Indeed, I had already seen it happen: one of the guys who used to travel to Smethwick in Bollo's car not so many years previously had managed to get himself banged up for armed robbery. If it could happen to a guy who'd shown such promise, how much easier for kids who were at a loose end all the time?

With my profile now higher than it had ever been, I was asked to give occasional motivational talks at school assemblies, and to address young black and Asian groups about how they might achieve more. I don't know whether I inspired anyone, but the experience got me thinking about the ways in which cricket had given me a passport to a wider world, and a degree of self-confidence that many of my schoolmates had lacked – certainly when taken out of their familiar surroundings. It was something that I'd give more and more thought to over the next few years.

In October I had a date in London. The team was invited to Buckingham Palace to receive our Championship medals from the Duke of Edinburgh. The lads were all speculating about whether the Duke might make one of his famous gaffes. Belly was offering odds that he'd look at us two and ask us which tribe we belonged to. In the end, however, His Royal Highness disappointed us, breezing through the ceremony without a single glitch. There was another plaudit that autumn when a Birmingham-based firm of solicitors named me Warwickshire's Most Improved Young Player of 1995. Although not exactly a royal seal of approval, it was a personal accolade, and because it came from people who knew a bit more about me and the game locally it meant a lot.

It was around this time that I embarked on one of the more serious relationships I'd had so far. After Parvaz's death I felt very down, and a friend introduced me to a lovely bright

CHAPTER 14 : SWINGS AND ROUNDABOUTS

girl called Deena. She was mixed race, being half Egyptian. The fact that she was Muslim would have cut little ice with my family: yes, they would have liked her, and it would be nice that they shared her beliefs, but such was the close-knit structure of our community that she would have been considered as much an outsider as if she'd been white. Here was the double-edged nature of our life in Small Heath: it offered great support, but was essentially inward-looking. There was in any case something of a gulf between me and Deena in terms of upbringing. She came from a professional family, had had a private education and was at ease in all kinds of situations. Like a lot of people from the best schools, she could swear like a trooper, which always struck me as funny. Anyway, all this was academic really, because I hid our relationship from the family, ducking and diving and being a 'secret Asian' – something I'd seen other guys doing over the years – and hoping they never found out. It's not that I was in any way ashamed, just that I didn't want them to worry, which I knew they would do if they found out. This would probably seem crazy to a white British family, but we youngsters from Small Heath were very new to this country, or rather our parents were, and very unsure of ourselves. We always put our families' feelings very high on the agenda. From a practical point of view, my having a girlfriend from outside our community would have placed a real strain on my mother, whose English was almost non-existent. And what if we'd decided to marry and have a family? What problems would our children have faced? In the end, I let the affair fizzle out. My family and my community had given me so much; when push came to shove I was reluctant to break with convention.

Despite my worries about the family, and the shock of losing Parvaz, I had a lot to feel good about that winter, and once I'd had a rest I couldn't wait for April to come, so that I could pick up where I left off in September. But before that I had a foreign trip. In February I was asked by my old friend Raja Khan to join a party of Birmingham school children who were embarking on a trip to India and Pakistan. The pretext was cricket – and I was to undertake coaching duties – but the underlying aim was to show these kids, all but two of whom had Asian backgrounds, what life was like in the country their parents once called home. Raja himself had made such a trip at 16, and always said that it had the most amazing impact on him: it educated him about what life was really like back there, but more importantly gave him a profound sense of appreciation – even

CHAPTER 14 : SWINGS AND ROUNDABOUTS

gratitude – for what he had in the UK. For him it had been voyage of self – discovery, and this was what he hoped to pass on to our party of teenage boys.

All but one of the group had been born in the UK. Just about all of them had one or both parents born in the sub – continent. For most of them it was their first trip. We flew into Islamabad, and drove up to Mirpur, home to so many thousands of Birmingham's Pakistanis. There we visited a cousin of Raja's who'd raised seven kids in the UK and taken them all back there to live a more traditional life among his extended family. This cousin demonstrated the strength and depth of his ties, showing us a wall-hanging of his family tree, which he could trace back three or four hundred years and even further. This, he reflected, was what was breaking down in so many western societies. And he stressed the point to the young boys, that the danger in Britain is that if you fail economically you can slip into an under-class. Back home that wouldn't necessarily happen. There's no sophisticated welfare system, but there is a huge depth of support from the densely inter-woven family networks.

While the children absorbed the images and sounds of Asian life, I revisited first my father's home and then my mother's village. That was still the place I liked best. The people had so little, but seemed so contented, so welcoming.

We moved on to India, which was new territory for me. In Bombay we all saw the terrible divide between the wealthy and the poor. It was so stark that some of the boys, observing the ragged beggars from the window of their taxi, even as they sped past luxury hotels and elegant gardens, admitted that they were scared of going out. It wasn't that they thought they would be in danger – they all felt at ease out there, a part of the place – but they had no idea how they would cope with the diseased, the crippled, the blind who were everywhere, living in the streets and begging for scraps.

Like most of us, they didn't know how to react.

But we were here for cricket, and with World Cup fever raging the kids had the chance to visit the ground where India would shortly play Australia. Here they were privileged to have a quick bowl in the nets against the world's greatest players before settling down to enjoy the game. It was a real whistle – stop tour. From Bombay we moved on to Kashmir and visited a refugee camp, handing out gifts. Not food, not clothing, but bats and balls and caps. So much was crowded into a scant fortnight.

CHAPTER 14 : SWINGS AND ROUNDABOUTS

After Kashmir it was Karachi and a brief encounter with the one guy they all wanted to meet, Wasim Akram, in town for the match between Pakistan and England.

In Lahore there was a game at one of the great Pakistani public schools, the country's very own Eton. The kids were getting some terrific insights into a world that for most of them was just a figment of their parents' memory. Now it was real: the poverty, the wealth, the history and culture, the callss to prayer, the rich and poor bathing in the rivers, the colourful street markets, the bullock carts, the evident spirituality of the people and the remarkable cheerfulness in the face of so much want.

For me, here was another nudge in a direction I would one day take: being involved with youngsters not only as a teacher of cricketing technique, but also as a mentor, a sort of older brother figure. I had had guys like Paul Kenna back in the old neighbourhood, and Raja Khan; later I had had senior players like Paul Smith at Warwickshire who would take the trouble to seek me out and see how I was coping with the ups and downs of the professional cricketer's career. Now, at the tender age of 25 or so, I was myself able to offer a bit of advice and guidance to the younger ones. It seemed a good thing to be doing.

Back home the new season kicked off with a game at Cambridge. Those early-season fixtures against the universities are seen by some people as a bit of a joke, but they have traditionally given batsmen a chance to play themselves into form at the expense of bowling that really isn't up to first-class standard. Was I complaining? Not after I'd racked up a nice ton in my first innings of the year, sharing an opening stand of 228 with Nick Knight, and then suffering the indignity of being run out by a guy called Russell Cake – a direct hit from cover. It was a hell of a throw, and, looking back, my biggest regret is that I didn't have the presence of mind to say 'crumbs!'

I followed this start with a couple of poor performances, and I mean poor. It wasn't just a case of getting out; I didn't even feel good when I was at the crease. In my mind I tried to think my way back into the frame of mind I'd had the previous year when everything had been going so well. I tried to engender some of the passion we'd all felt then. But somehow the events of the winter still hung over me. As well as that I was feeling a bit disgruntled that I hadn't been offered a county cap. Against Sussex at Hove I got a scratchy 19 in the first innings and hoped to build on it in the second, but thanks to Nick Knight's awesome 100 before

CHAPTER 14 : SWINGS AND ROUNDABOUTS

lunch on the first day, plus big hundreds from Penney (134) and Reeve (168) we racked up 645 for 7 declared and didn't have to bat again, wrapping the match up by an innings.

Phil Neale was concerned about my loss of form, and more than that, my loss of zest for the game. He worked hard with me in the nets and at fielding, but I think he could tell my heart wasn't in it just now. Nevertheless, he was positive: all I needed was one decent score and everything was bound to click into place. For some reason, however, it just didn't work for me. Something had happened to my appetite.

In May I was dropped from the first team. I should have been devastated, but I wasn't. I knew I needed time out to think about where the problem lay and how I was going to deal with it. Maybe it was complacency. Okay, there was no county cap, but I had signed a two-year contract at the end of the previous season. Was it that, having worked so hard and withstood so many disappointments to get into the first team, there was just nothing left in the tank once my form deserted me?

Even as I chewed on it, the problem evaporated. Almost as suddenly as things had gone wrong, that magical, elusive thing called self-confidence started flowing through my veins once more. And with it came that other intangible thing, form. I have no idea why, but suddenly I started seeing the ball early and seeing it big. I started feeling the old buzz that came with smacking it across the practice field. I was still trying to work out what had gone wrong, and why, when I went out to bat in a three-dayer against Leicestershire seconds. It all fell into place, and I scored a fluent 170-odd. It seemed a bizarre reversal of fortune, so much so that I still doubted myself. Maybe I'd just got lucky. Maybe this was a flash in the pan. But in the second innings the improved form continued. I went out and did it all over again. 156. Suddenly I was feeling powerful, capable, fit and confident, supremely confident. I was ready to resume my first-team career. Unfortunately, it was too late for the fixture I would dearly love to have played in, against the touring Pakistanis. We won that by seven wickets. Once again, Anurag was preferred to me, scoring four in the first and nine in the second. Yes, I noticed; and yes, it hurt. Anurag clearly had a lot of ability, but I always felt that, like a lot of academic types, he spent too much time analysing his game rather than just getting on with it. One day his problem was that his bat was too heavy; a few weeks later it was too light; and so on.

CHAPTER 14 : SWINGS AND ROUNDABOUTS

These considerations were far from my mind right now, though. I knew I was ready to return to the first team, and Phil Neale obviously felt the same. He phoned me at home, congratulated me on my two tons and told me to pack my bags. Nick Knight had been called up for the England squad, and I would step back up for the game at Gloucestershire. As I drove down to Cheltenham I was raring to go. They may have had Courtney Walsh in their team, a bowler we all respected – or feared – but I was back at my best. What did I have to worry about?

When I woke up in my hotel room on the morning of the game, I felt focussed and strong. It was the first time I'd had that sense of well-being since the game at Cambridge. All it needed was for Tim Munton to win the toss. He was captaining the side since Dermot, after a few indifferent performances on the field, had taken the unusual step of dropping himself. You have to respect a guy who can do that. Tim was an altogether different character, a quiet, thoughtful, family man rather than the verbally aggressive party animal that Dermot was. I was out having a net on the morning of the game when I saw him walking purposefully towards me. He was still 30 or 40 yards from me when I said out loud, 'Oh no, you're joking!' No captain ever walks over to you like that before a game unless it's bad news.

'Waz, I'm sorry mate but we're going to play Anurag instead of you.' I didn't say anything. I couldn't think of anything to say. I was too busy with the chaos of thoughts rampaging around my head. With the benefit of hindsight I can see that I should have have made it more difficult for him. Other players – not all of them, but a few I've known – would have argued the toss. In my shoes they would have thrown the previous game up in Tim's face. How can you drop a guy who's just passed 150 twice in the same match? Don't you know that was the first time a Warwickshire player has ever done that in the county's entire history? It might not have got me anywhere this time, but it would make it that bit harder next time around. Given a choice between dropping some member of the awkward squad as against a nice guy who took it lying down, I know who I'd choose. But I wasn't like that then. When it came right down to it I was meek and mild. Maybe I was being typically Asian, grateful just to be there. My friend Asif Din was the same, he once told me. He just accepted it all with a shrug and a smile and everyone always said what a nice guy he was.

CHAPTER 14 : SWINGS AND ROUNDABOUTS

Later I would feel genuine anger, but when Tim gave me the hard word I just felt gobsmacked. He stood there for a moment as if he was waiting for me to say something. But there were no words there. He turned to walk away. As he went he looked over his shoulder at me. 'Sorry,' he said, and carried on to the pavilion, leaving me to work out which feeling to deal with first, because now they were milling around in my head: anger, hurt, astonishment, bitterness, envy, disgust. A couple of days later there was another one: grim satisfaction, because the team proceeded to bat horribly, twice in the match, and got stuffed by an innings and 116. I'd be a liar if I said I didn't take something from that.

I got back in the side a week or two later, but I kicked of in the worst possible style with a duck against Durham, bowled by a beauty, first ball from Simon Brown. It was classic 'jaffa', pitching on leg and swinging out to take my off stump. There was nothing I could do about it. It just happened. I was sweating on a decent score now, well aware that a single unlucky break could send me back into exile for weeks, maybe months. Mercifully, it came good for me in the second dig. I got off to a cracking start. Coming in at the fall of the first wicket, I waltzed down the pitch to a left-arm spinner and hit a straight six, following up with a similar shot off the next ball which bounced just inside the rope. My 50 was up in 61 balls and before I knew it I was on 98, pouncing on a nice half-volley on leg stump to take three through mid-wicket. I totalled 130 out of 361 for 9 declared as we went on to win the game by a massive 282 runs. It was my first 100 at Edgbaston.

A lot of people will tell you that your second season in county cricket is harder than your first. Opposing players, they say, will work out your weaknesses. That may be so, but I didn't feel it applied to me. As far as I was concerned if I was getting dismissed cheaply it was because I was playing badly. I blamed myself. And now, after the hundred against Durham, I hit a bit of a lean patch: nought and 8 against Glamorgan; a 50 and a 40 against Worcestershire; nought and 14 at the Oval. Even when I got myself in twice against Worcestershire I didn't manage to push on. When we came back from the Surrey game, however, everything fell into place once more. We were playing Essex. They had a decent attack: Mark Ilott, Ronnie Irani, Peter Such and Ashley Cowan, with Graham Gooch ready to help out if necessary. They had us 20 for 4 at one stage, but I stuck in there and very nearly managed the unusual feat

CHAPTER 14 : SWINGS AND ROUNDABOUTS

of carrying my bat before being last out having scored 126 out of 253. It was nice to bring the hundred up by hitting off – spinner Peter Such for a juicy six over mid – on. Pity about the result, though. In their second innings Essex built on Gooch's 127th century to reach 450 for 6, leaving us an unlikely 400 or so to win. When your number one gets himself out for another duck, it's always going to be hard work. We were stuffed, by 170 runs.

Just as I thought things were on the up, they were about to take a turn for the worse. Derbyshire, away. For some reason they were one of my bogey teams. And, like most players, I hated playing at their ground. It was ugly, lacking in atmosphere, and generally freezing cold. I just never performed against them there, and this game was no exception. I batted twice and scored a measly 1 in the first innings, 8 in the second. Not a happy memory.

The season wound up with a home game against Lancashire. We topped 300 in both innings, my contribution being 6 and 32. Lanes rattled up 597 (Fairbrother 204, Lloyd 113), but the weather intervened and that was that.

CHAPTER 15

'Thought you dark fellers could run!'

WHATEVER kind of season you've had – and mine had been patchy at best – if you've got an overseas contract you can soon start looking forward to better times. This winter I was Down Under again, not in Oz but in New Zealand. Welchy had put me on to a club called Petone Riverside, and they'd made me an acceptable offer. They'd had Jeremy Snape (Northants, Gloucester and Leicestershire) the previous season and even arranged for me to stay with the same people, a lovely couple called Darren and Trina who put me up in their bungalow about five minutes from the ground and treated me as family.

Welchy and I decided to travel out together and this time break the journey. I hated those long direct flights, and we had an invitation from Dermot to call in at Hong Kong where his father lived and worked, being headmaster of a public school.

I said goodbye to my family at the beginning of October. I felt guiltier than

CHAPTER 15 : 'THOUGHT YOU DARK FELLERS COULD RUN!'

ever about leaving them. I realised I was spending less and less time with them, but I didn't see any alternative. I had to earn a living throughout the year, and cricket was my trade. If I'd applied myself at school, maybe I would have had some alternative way of making my way, but I hadn't. Luckily for me, at this time my Mum had other things on her mind. She was getting more and more anxious about my sister. Raheena was now in her mid-twenties and still single. It wasn't what my parents' generation had grown up to expect. As it happened, just when Mum was starting to talk about going back to Pakistan to look for a suitable husband for her, my sister met someone through Mum that she really liked and announced that they would be getting married in December, while I was on the other side of the world.

New Zealand proved to be a different proposition from Australia. The weather wasn't at all the same. It rained a lot, and it rained heavily, and Wellington lived up to its name, the windy city. The pitches we played on were green and lush, perfectly suited to the local bowlers who all seemed to come from the same production line, serving up little dobbers – medium-paced balls that moved around in the air and off the surface. Our ground was quite picturesque. There were mountains in the distance and plenty of trees around us – but no sight-screens, so you frequently had a job spotting the ball as it came in against a dark backdrop.

Day to day, life was a lot quieter than in Sydney or Melbourne, which was probably a good thing on balance. I coached at the club a couple of days a week, did a lot of reading, and otherwise concentrated on cricket, calling Phil Neale every so often to update him on my progress. Being a city boy, however, I found life there just a bit too staid, and started to feel quite homesick. It hit me particularly hard when Mum and Raheena took off to Pakistan for the wedding while I was stuck in Wellington with only the delights of a rainy South Island Sunday to keep me amused. Not for the first time, I was glad I have never been a drinker. A stint out there would have driven many a young guy down to the pub.

Socially we did our best. There were a number of other English guys out there, such as former England bowlers Paul Jarvis and Neil Mallender, Kevin Innes from Northants and Alex Wharf from Glamorgan. England were touring that winter, and I was able to catch up with Knighty when they came to town. I was delighted to find out that a mate of mine, Aftab Habib, was playing at a place called Nelson, three hours

CHAPTER 15 : 'THOUGHT YOU DARK FELLERS COULD RUN!'

away from where we were staying, so one way or another I had a few contacts to break up what was a pretty undemanding schedule. A couple of days a week a few of us would drop in at an Indian restaurant in town and I'd bullshit my way through the menu. And then at the weekend we'd go down to The Dive, the Diva nightclub, and after the boys had put away their usual gallon or so of beer I'd drive them home.

But it was hardly life in the fast lane. As in Australia we only played once a week, the games spread over two weekends, with each side allowed 96 overs. This meant that as an opener you had time to build an innings, but it only took one wet weekend for you to be woefully short of match practice. There was also a three to four-week break over the Christmas period, so I decided to put the free time to good use and hop across to Australia.

I had a lot of friends by now in Sydney and Melbourne. I'd played with Stuart MacGill, the Aussie leg-spinner, at North Perth a couple of years previously; he was now playing Sheffield Shield cricket for New South Wales. Even better, my old mate Raja Khan was in Sydney as assistant manager to the touring Pakistani Test team. God knows how he got that job, but, as I said earlier, the guy was well connected. He knew all the angles. He'd even managed to do the hard sell on Wasim Akram and become his agent. We always said he'd sell a bucket with a hole in it, and he'd excelled himself this time. He'd gone the distance educationally too, studying for a PhD, so he wouldn't have had much trouble talking his way into this job. As well as him there was Mushtaq Mohammed, who of course I knew from Warwickshire; he was now coaching the national team.

When I told Raja I was coming across he contacted Mushy who insisted I came and stayed with the Pakistani team at the Sheraton Hotel. I arrived there to find it was fully booked, but Mushy got an extra bed moved into his room for me. He and the team were in town preparing for a one-dayer against the host nation on New Year's Day. It was part of a triangular series with the Windies. The venue was the legendary SCG. My last memory of the Sydney Cricket Ground was sitting on the Hill watching England take on the Aussies in the fifth Test in 1991.

The morning after I checked in, the team were just leaving when Mushy told me to follow him. I would travel with them to the ground. I can't say I felt comfortable about that at all. My instant reaction was to back away. I'd just be in the way. The players

CHAPTER 15 : 'THOUGHT YOU DARK FELLERS COULD RUN!'

would have had enough of people hanging around at the hotel. With the game just 24 hours away they would want to be alone or just with each other. However, I had played against guys like Akram, Waqar and Mushtaq Ahmed, so they were very welcoming and insisted I get on the team bus.

While the guys practised, I strolled around the famous old ground, looking in at the museum and checking out all the Bradman memorabilia. I loved reading about that guy. In 1991 I'd made a pilgrimage to his home town of Bowral. As I stood and looked at one of his baggy green caps in the display case I remembered how I'd heard about him years ago on the streets of Birmingham. I don't know who first told us about him, but we all grew up knowing that there was this legendary guy called The Don who'd averaged over 99 in Test matches. Later I'd read how he used to practise batting by hitting a golf ball with a stump, hour after hour under the merciless Australian sun. What an inspiration.

Practice finished at about 3pm and the players all headed back to the hotel to rest in preparation for the game next day. They were remarkably relaxed. I think it was a case of confidence, of knowing how good they were and being quite sure they could put on a decent performance when the time came. Wasim Akram, the captain, was the most relaxed, singing along to all the Punjabi songs that were being played over the sound system on the team bus.

The Pakistani team, at least in my time in cricket, has always been seen as something of an enigma. Pound for pound they are probably the most talented bunch of cricketers around. They have the hunger and the fighting spirit to beat anyone on their day, but unfortunately they lack unity at crucial times. My observation is that they seem as individuals to get into a comfort zone so that they need real adversity – or a kick up the backside – to produce their best. Pakistani players, like the Pakistani people, have always worn their hearts on their sleeves, and whenever someone throws down a challenge, that's when the passion – and with it the performance – comes to the surface. They've all grown up in the fiercely competitive domestic leagues, and many have emerged from the deprived inner cities. No one's going to tell them they don't deserve to be up there competing with the world's best. They're proud to be there, honoured too, but they absolutely believe they have the right to be there.

Speaking as a guy of Punjabi extraction, I would say we tend to be very passionate,

CHAPTER 15 : 'THOUGHT YOU DARK FELLERS COULD RUN!'

hugely patriotic, but we also have a chaotic streak. You can see it in our day to day lives among our families and within our neighbourhoods. If someone wants to tell you something he'll more than likely stand there and shout right in your face, an attribute the British find particularly hard to get used to. Other people will join in and before you know where you are you're having three or four conversations at once, most of them revolving around somebody who's just died back in Pakistan, how kids don't listen to adults any more… and weddings, of course. A stranger would assume there was a major row going on, with violence about to break out. But no, people just get involved, and give it everything they've got. It's a kind of street theatre. Only the previous September, before I flew out, I'd seen a classic example of the sort of thing I'm talking about. One of our neighbours got burgled. It was in the middle of the night. The father of the family woke up, and there was this thief rummaging through the drawers, right beside the bed with his wife fast asleep next to him. He leapt out of bed, the thief ran for it, and there's this guy in his Y-fronts and string vest chasing the malefactor down the street, shouting and screaming. Heroic stuff, but then the neighbours started waking up, throwing open their windows and wanting to know what was going on. Within a matter of minutes half the neighbourhood was out on the street. This was four o'clock in the morning, the thief had disappeared, but everybody was dashing to and fro in different directions. Nobody had a clue who they were chasing, but they all joined in, and they all yelled at the top of their voices. When they realised the bird had flown they had shouted arguments in the middle of the street about what they would have done if they had caught him. Perhaps we're all a lot of drama queens.

The morning of the game the players gathered in the hotel foyer. Play wasn't due to start until 2.30 as it was a day-night fixture. During the night Raja had had some terrible news. His mother had died, and he was returning to the UK immediately. I knew her well as a neighbour and friend, so it was a huge shock to me too. I couldn't help wondering what my family would be going through at the loss of one of the community so soon after Parvaz's death. All I could do was offer Raja my condolences and watch him leave for the airport.

I travelled to the ground with the team, deep in thought. Around me everyone seemed in a relaxed frame of mind. As the bus approached the stadium we could see

CHAPTER 15 : 'THOUGHT YOU DARK FELLERS COULD RUN!'

the crowds already gathering. Before we got off Mushtaq said a few words of encouragement and there was the usual brief prayer. Then everybody wished each other luck and headed for the dressing-rooms.

An hour or two later, as the players returned to the pavilion from their warm-up routines and fielding drills, Mushtaq came over and said he wanted a word with me. The team were coming to the end of a long tour, he said, and quite a few of them were suffering from niggling little injuries. Basically, they were short of fit players and had no one to do 12th man duties. I remember looking at Mushy, absolutely dumb-struck, wondering whether he was about to ask me what I thought he was going to ask. I heard him say he'd spoken to Wasim Akram and they'd both wondered whether I could step in and help the boys out. I could hardly believe what I was hearing. In part I was overcome at the prospect of taking the field in an international match, but mainly I was struggling to work out how a side of their standing could be so depleted as to require help from a foreigner who just happened to drop by. Okay, I was of the same blood as these guys, but my passport was British and my ambition had always been to play for England one day. Pakistan had never entered my calculations. And here they were asking me to be 12th man. Thirty years ago that would have been a polite way of conning me into bringing the drinks out, but in modern one-day cricket, and knowing the way Pakistan played, I was pretty sure that one or other of their players – certainly their bowlers – would trot off the field at some stage, so there was every prospect of me taking part.

I jumped at the chance. I would've been crazy not to. There was of course the small matter of me not having any kit, but in the dressing-room the guys sorted me out. One of the injured, fast bowler Mohammed Zahid, gave me his shirt and trousers. Saeed Anwar dug a spare pair of boots out of his bag, and some socks, and I was all set. It seemed an odd way to prepare for an international fixture, but I wasn't going to complain. I sat in the dressing-room, unable to believe what was happening to me. I was then privileged to witness a team-talk, Pakistani style. They had lost the toss and would be fielding, so this was a chance to see how a top international side planned to deal with a frighteningly strong Aussie batting line-up. At Warwickshire or Sussex it would have involved a detailed discussion of each player's strengths or weaknesses, with the guys chipping in from all sides. This was rather different.

CHAPTER 15 : 'THOUGHT YOU DARK FELLERS COULD RUN!'

Wasim Akram: 'Right boys, Mark Waugh. Keep it off his legs, he's good through there.'

Waqar Younis: 'Leave him to me.'

Wasim: 'Okay. Right, what about Ponting?'

Waqar: 'I'll sort him out.'

Wasim: 'That right-hander who bats at number four...' He meant Greg Blewett, but none of them could pronounce the guy's name.

And so it went on – but not for very long. They spent no time going through their opponents' weaknesses. That didn't seem the important thing. Preparation was all down to rekindling their belief in their own ability. And that belief was absolute. If they played to the best of their ability, they would win. Simple as that.

The team talk was followed by the usual short prayer conducted by Saqlain Mushtaq, and out they went. I went out onto the balcony with the injured Saeed Anwar. Like me he was a left-hand opening bat, so we had a fair bit to talk about. Saeed wanted to know what it was like playing in the English County Championship. He fancied giving it a try, but was worried that he didn't have the necessary physique. He'd noticed how well developed the Aussies were, and had made up his mind to start weight training when he got back home. He stressed one thing to me about opening, that you should impose yourself on the bowlers, face up to them and not let them bully you.

Pakistan got off to a decent start with Wasim Akram making inroads into the Australian batting. But all the time as I watched I only really had one thing on my mind. Would I get onto the field? It seemed unlikely as the overs ticked down, and at around the 35 mark I resigned myself to the fact that I'd had my moment of glory, just being selected as 12th man. With 10 overs to go Australia were struggling with Shane Warne and Tom Moody holding things together. I'd just watched Wasim bowl the last of his overs when I saw him signal to the dressing-room. Before I had a chance to figure out what he wanted he'd thrown his sweater over his shoulder and was trudging off the field. He was going to put his feet up for the rest of the innings. I wiped my hands on my trousers and raced down the stairs. As I passed Wasim and made my way to backward point he grinned at me. 'Good luck,' he said. 'Enjoy it!'

One thing I hadn't anticipated was the level of noise out there in the middle. I knew it would be loud, but it was nothing like anything I'd experienced before with the crowd in party mode, shouting

CHAPTER 15 : 'THOUGHT YOU DARK FELLERS COULD RUN!'

encouragement to their batsmen and abuse at the outfielders. Before I had time to take it all in, however, the ball was flying towards me. It came at a nice height, first bounce, and I was able to gather it cleanly and return it right over the stumps. I immediately felt a surge of confidence. I did this sort of thing week in week out for club and county. It was my profession. Why should a routine piece of fielding be any different just because we were at the SCG with 40,000 half-naked fans celebrating every Aussie run with another can of beer? I found out soon enough, when I chased a ball to the boundary and failed to catch it. Immediately I heard the shout, 'Thought you dark fellers could run, mate!' Just in case I hadn't heard him he and his mates shook up their tinnies and gave me a nice shower of foam.

With Australia approaching the climax of their innings Moin Khan, who'd taken over as captain when Wasim went off, spread the field, signalling for me to drop back to deep third man. As I headed down there a huge Mexican wave broke out right around the ground. I stood there with my back to the crowd as cups, plastic bottles and all sorts of rubbish flew past me. It was pretty harmless stuff, and I did my best to ignore it. I remembered participating in a similar sort of thing myself when I was a spectator on the Hill four or five years before, so I could hardly complain. I had seen life from both sides of the fence now. Hillites are part of the colour of cricket. They pay good money to be entertained and expect to have a good time.

The innings closed with Australia on 292 for 7. I headed back to the dressing-room, aglow with pride and satisfaction as I rehearsed what I was going to say to the lads back in Small Heath. With my job done, I was now able to relax and watch as Pakistan chased a decent target under the lights. I sat chatting to Wasim Akram about his approach as an opening bowler. What he said perfectly reflected what I'd seen in the dressing-room earlier: a total reliance on self-belief and very little real thought about tactics or game plans. That approach, I suspected, was for us mere mortals. Wasim was a seriously deceptive bowler, coming in off quite a short run but hustling the ball through with an incredibly quick action. At six feet four, and with his broad shoulders, he had immense power. He could bowl six different deliveries an over, and it was this unpredictability that made him so lethal.

Wasim is also a charismatic figure, and that worked both for and against him. During the 1996 World Cup in Pakistan he found himself surrounded by religious

CHAPTER 15 : 'THOUGHT YOU DARK FELLERS COULD RUN!'

people at the hotel where he was staying, all of them insisting he should remove the earring he'd taken to wearing. To him it was just a personal adornment that meant nothing, but, as they told him, he was a national icon now, and should realise that everything he did set an example, and a man wearing jewellery was not approved of by the elders. This was difficult for Wasim. He was quite westernised now after all his years playing in the Championship and living in Lancashire, and apart from being a cricketer he was his own man – but that's the responsibility that goes with being a superstar in Pakistan.

Out on the field, Ijaz Ahmed played the crucial innings, scoring 123. Inzamam ul Haq weighed in with 59, and Pakistan inched across the line with seven down and one ball to spare. Back in the dressing-room the players discussed the game and their own performances light-heartedly. They had played well and they were happy. What was obvious to me was that above anything else they set out to enjoy their cricket. They delighted in each other's company and simply didn't worry too much about their own status.

I was all set, after the game, to go back to the hotel, but Wasim and Mushtaq had other thoughts. Why didn't I take a few of the boys out and practise one or two fielding techniques, like the sliding pick-up? To be honest I was amazed that a Test side needed this sort of practice, but of course I jumped at the chance to have a session with them. I think the whole thing was more a tribute to Warwickshire's reputation as a red-hot fielding side rather than to my own ability, which was modest but improving. What I noticed straight away, though, was that these guys were nowhere near as supple as they'd need to be to play. Wasim and Mushtaq of course had plenty of experience on England's well-grassed fields, and recognised that, coming from a hot dry country with threadbare outfields baked hard by the sun, the Pakistanis were way behind most other teams in this aspect of the game.

Back at the hotel the team's thoughts were naturally turning to Brisbane and the next game in the series. Mushtaq asked me if I wanted to travel on with the boys and do 12th-man duties again, but I felt I'd be intruding. I wasn't a Test player and I didn't belong in that exalted company. I'd had my 15 minutes of fame and it was nice to be asked, but I needed to re-enter my own world.

When the boys had moved on, I spent a day with Stuart MacGill, who was over in Sydney for the game. We'd played together for North Perth for a couple of seasons in the

CHAPTER 15 : 'THOUGHT YOU DARK FELLERS COULD RUN!'

early nineties and become good mates. I've often noticed that batsmen and bowlers make good friends. Batsmen are more likely to see each other as a potential competitors for a place and are that much more guarded, and I'm sure the same applies to bowlers. I had a lot of time for Stuey. You had to feel sorry for a fine practitioner who had the misfortune to be playing his cricket at the same time as the legendary Shane Warne. Even so, he's managed to take many wickets, and it's been good to see him spinning his magic for Nottinghamshire in recent years.

The rest of my holiday in Oz I spent between Sydney and Melbourne. I wanted to get across to Perth to see a couple of old mates but the distances were always going to be too great. Perth is one of my favourite places Down Under: the weather is consistently warm and so are the people. I'd spent a couple of winters there playing and coaching and it suited me. The only trouble is that it's a hell of a long way from anywhere else. It's a shorter flight north to Jakarta, the capital of Indonesia, than it is to Sydney. Not many people know that, but if you've ever travelled to Perth from New South Wales you'll be ready to believe it.

It was soon time, in any case, to resume my duties in New Zealand. As I flew back to Wellington I thought about my moment in the spotlight with the Pakistani team. It meant more than I ever thought it would. As youngsters back in Small Heath we'd all talked about the Pakistani team as if they were gods. And now I had rubbed shoulders with them on the field of play. Yes, I was 25 and a professional cricketer; I was no longer a scruffy school-kid playing in the street with a home-made bat, but when I was on the field with Waqar and Wasim and the other guys I think that little boy was there beside me, totally in awe and feeling mightily blessed to be among his heroes. I now found myself wondering what the differences were between them and me, what separated an average county player from an international star, and all I could think of was what I'd seen in that dressing-room, an absolute lack of fear. They feared no opponent, and they certainly didn't worry about failure. They went out onto the field with heads held high, walking with a little swagger, and a supreme confidence in their ability. I knew, in my heart, that I had let the uncertainties of the professional game make me wary, and perhaps that was where I was failing.

CHAPTER 16

Warwickshire: the end of an era

IN MARCH I flew home to a new domestic season, determined to establish myself as a fixture in the Warwickshire side and kick on. But 1997 got off to the worst possible start in our opener against Glamorgan: 6 in the first innings and nought in the second. Fair enough, it wasn't the greatest opening-day performance, but I was shocked to find I was dropped for the next game. If everyone was demoted after one bad game you'd never get a settled side. I'd finished the previous season on a high, and although I'd failed with the bat in this first game we'd hardly distinguished ourselves collectively as batsmen or bowlers, totalling 151 and 77 for 3 against a Glamorgan total of 551 for 3 declared.

I think this was where the first seeds of real doubt were planted in my mind about my future with the county. The fact that I could apparently establish myself in the side and then be dropped after just one dodgy game suggested that I was still nowhere near being secure. Warwickshire had been my life since I was 12. And my devotion to the bear and ragged staff had dated from even earlier, when I'd carved the letters WCCC on my home-made bat. Did they have any idea how much the county meant to me?

My problem now was that Andy Moles and Nick Knight had the two opening positions, and they were a class act, no doubt about it. Was I going to have to hope for injuries, or for Nick to be called up to the England squad? That wasn't the way I wanted to live out my professional career, relying on other people's failures or injuries.

I had a heart to heart with Nick. I could trust the guy, and I respected his judgement. Okay, we were both openers, but I was no threat to him. He was an England player and could take a more detached view. I confided in him that it had finally crossed my mind that I might move on at the end of the season. I didn't want to, but I was certain I could get regular first-team cricket somewhere else. I'm sure Nick only had my interests at heart when he mentioned to one or two of the senior players that I was getting frustrated, so much so that I was considering a move. The next thing I knew I was called to a meeting with Phil Neale and told in no uncertain terms that if that was

CHAPTER 16 : WARWICKSHIRE: THE END OF AN ERA

the case I should understand that it was only right for the county to pick players who were guaranteed to be around next year. Without meaning to, I'd set events in motion. Now it looked as though there was no turning back.

But, as ever, that rag of hope was held out to me. If I carried on scoring for the seconds, Phil told me, I would be considered for selection. I was back there again, and I knew what to do. Get my head down and play, which is precisely what I did. After that little chat my next five innings brought me 58, 102, 106, 45 and 210. Okay, I thought, let's see what happens now, with Nick away on international duty. Nothing: that's what happened. I remained in the second team. But in a sense it didn't really matter quite as much now as it might have done. Finally, my heart was hardening. I knew I was good enough, and I knew that my face no longer fitted. I was playing as much to put myself in the shop window as to impress my own employers.

By the time I got the call from Phil Neale, I had more or less resigned myself to moving on. He rang one Friday afternoon. I was sitting in a Worcester restaurant with Scotty, a mate of mine, having a chat about options for next season. Mark Scott was an ex-Worcestershire and Sussex player who'd moved into coaching and had a strong reputation as someone that pros could turn to for one-on-one sessions. He'd spent a lot of time nurturing a young Vikram Solanki. He was a top coach who, with a bit of luck, could and should have been involved with the country's elite. Scotty had a good network of contacts and he told me he was willing to ask around for me. We were drinking coffee when the phone rang. It was Phil. I'd been selected to play in a televised Sunday League game at Durham. To be honest I was taken aback. Scotty thought it was funny. He lifted the tablecloth and peered underneath it, theatrically. 'You sure they haven't got this place bugged?' he said. 'Soon as you mention leaving they want you back in the side.'

I had presumed I was off the radar as far as Phil was concerned. Still, if he wanted me I'd be there. I was busy calling around to see who else was going and what the arrangements were when Phil rang again and told me to have a word with Dougie Brown. I could travel up with him. Three-quarters of an hour later came a third call. 'I'm really sorry, Waz. There's been a change of plan. Look, it's out of my hands and it's been decided to give Anurag a run out.'

It was clear from Phil's tone that he was the unwilling bearer of bad news. The

CHAPTER 16 : WARWICKSHIRE: THE END OF AN ERA

decision had obviously come from other sources. But then things were in a state of flux that year. Nick Knight, Andy Moles and Neil Smith all captained the side at some stage; Tim Munton was missing, injured, all year, and Keith Piper missed half the season with an Achilles tendon problem. The management had plenty on their minds. Which begged the question: why had it never occurred to them to ask me to plug the gaps?

Although I was now prepared to face the inevitable, I was still sore about never having been granted a county cap. Dom Ostler, a good lad and someone I never had a problem with, had got one in his first year before he'd even made a Championship hundred. It all seemed a bit arbitrary, and that's putting it mildly, but there's never been a hard and fast rule about caps, and there have been countless anomalies over the years at every county. It tends to be regarded as something of an honour. In the dictionary of English cricket the words 'jobs' and 'for the boys' are never far apart on the page. Take Dermot Reeve. Opinions of his capabilities vary, but for me he would have been just the guy to take over as coach when Phil Neale finished. I never knew quite where I stood with Dermot, but the facts are there for all to see: as a captain he got the very best out of his players and the results during his reign reflect that. Nevertheless, when the time came he was overlooked in favour of John Inverarity, the former Aussie spin bowler, despite having captained the county through one of the most successful periods in its history.

We were now well into August and I had a lot on my mind. I was frantically trying to sort myself out with a new club. The rules say that you're not allowed to talk to other counties while you're still under contract, but in reality there's an awful lot of off-the-record conversations, and 'meetings-that-never-took-place', with the result that most of them have made up their minds about recruitment by mid-August. In my case I didn't think Warwickshire were going to lose any sleep over it. They'd written me off.

I'd had talks with four other clubs, among them Sussex. They'd suffered a mass exodus over the past couple of years, class players like Ian Salisbury, Ed Giddins, Colin and Alan Wells, and this season were bottom of just about everything. I quite fancied them. If things were that bad, surely I could get regular first-team cricket there, and from their current position there was only one way to go: upwards. I was pretty sure that I'd be an attractive proposition to them, coming as I did from a club that had ingrained in us the winning habit.

CHAPTER 16 : WARWICKSHIRE: THE END OF AN ERA

All the time I was doing this I felt a bit guilty, as if I was doing something wrong rather than just looking out for myself. So I was surprised when Dermot called me to say he'd been talking to Sussex and had recommended me to them. I never even realised he knew what was going on. But by this time he had announced that he was leaving at the end of the season to take up a coaching job at Somerset, so maybe he felt it was okay to bend the rules a bit. I also took Andy Moles into my confidence as he was a good mate of Tony Pigott, once a Sussex stalwart before he switched to Surrey, and now back on the south coast as their Chief Exec. I learned that Tony was looking to arrest the county's slide and bring in a bit of new blood. As it happened, Sussex were due to play a four-day game at Edgbaston, giving us an ideal opportunity to meet up. We talked in the physio room. It was all a bit furtive. I was really impressed with his ideas, and he was anxious to get a firm commitment from me so that he could go to his committee and 'sell' me. I told him I was up for it. I'd always liked playing at Hove, was impressed by him, and was desperate for regular first-team cricket.

At the same time I was getting interest from Worcestershire – all very good for my ego, but worrying at the same time. In some ways Worcester would have been a good move: it was nearby and I had plenty of friends there. I knew Alamgir Sheriyar, a fast bowler I'd played with in the various Warwickshire youth sides – in fact, he was delegated to approach me – and I knew guys like Stu Lampitt and David Leatherdale from the Birmingham League. It was an appealing prospect. On the other hand I really felt that at 25 I needed to make a move out of Birmingham and get away from home for a spell. The pressure to get married and settle down was increasing all the time, and I simply wasn't ready for that.

Westerners who deride the practice of arranged marriages don't really understand how much thought goes into the process of selecting a suitable partner for your son or daughter. Or should I say persistence? They should meet Asian families. They're always telling you about some nice girl or other they've been investigating, always from a good family, always well educated, and always 'ever so pretty, Wasim, just the kind you would like.' On one occasion Mum tried to interest me in a girl up in Scotland. She must have given her a hell of a build-up – either that or she caught me when my resistance was low. This one was really pretty, and not one of those little round dumpy creatures; she was tall, five foot seven at

CHAPTER 16 : WARWICKSHIRE: THE END OF AN ERA

least. She sounded interesting, so I decided I might as well follow this one up, partly out of curiosity, partly to appease Mum. I told her to let the girl's mother know that I would call her that evening. During the day I managed to get myself quite excited, imagining a sort of Muslim version of Angelina Jolie.

When I spoke to her, the girl of course had to pretend this was all a big surprise, as if her mother hadn't been chewing her ear about it all day too, so when I called I got a sort of shrieked 'my goodness!' How on earth had I managed to get her number? When she stopped acting like a soap star our conversation went quite well as we talked about life in general and what we did and where we lived, who our favourite film stars were and all that getting-to-know-you stuff. Somehow we decided that it would be nice to meet up, at which point it turned out that she had a job and travelling was a real hassle so rather than meeting me halfway at somewhere like Newcastle why didn't I fly up to Glasgow? For Angelina Jolie? Of course, no problem. This was sounding riskier by the minute.

After I'd agreed to go north I started to sober up in my thinking. As my mates said, Waz, what if she's a complete Barry Crocker? A what? You know – a total shocker, man. They had a point. I should have demanded a picture before I got this far. I asked Mum. Oh goodness gracious, that was going to be so difficult, but she would do her best. I was due to fly up on the Friday evening, and it was Wednesday already. After turning the house upside down she finally came up with something – a film of a wedding where this girl had been a guest. I slid it into the VCR and sat on the edge of my seat, hoping to be blown away, but secretly dreading the worst.

That's when I discovered that Mum hadn't really ever seen her, but she was sure she knew who she was… She stopped the tape and fetched one of my aunties in to point the girl out, and she brought a cousin or two with her and they all got their glasses out and sat around the TV. Raheena came in from work and joined in the fun. This was all terribly exciting – for them, so exciting that they had to make a pot of tea to calm themselves down. Finally, we were ready to roll.

'That's her!' my auntie shouted as the camera panned to a table where everyone was dining and chattering. 'What, that?' I half shouted, freezing the tape and rewinding it. 'That?' The statuesque beauty of my dreams was five foot nothing and – well, the kindest assessment would be 'not outstanding'. Angelina Jolie? More like Dom Joly.

CHAPTER 16 : WARWICKSHIRE: THE END OF AN ERA

Now I was in big trouble, because I'd booked my flight and made the arrangements. Worse than that, I'd told everyone of my plans. What should I do? My family knew straight away that I wasn't going to go. They could tell by the look on my face. Raheena was disgusted with me. She waded in before I'd said a word about maybe not going. She knew very well what I was thinking. 'It's the person you choose, not the looks! You men, you're so... shallow.' I told her I admired her stance, but I was the mug who was going to have to wake up every morning looking at this girl, and although I wasn't exactly Omar Sharif I had hoped for something a little more appealing.

Later that evening I plucked up my courage and concocted the most outrageous lie I could come up with. Then I called the girl. She was suitably distraught about the sudden death in my family, but a bit perplexed that I couldn't remember the guy's name. I was on the back foot from the start, but I managed to wriggle my way through the rest of the conversation and beat a retreat. I had to get online – fast. There was a £250 rebate waiting for me if I cancelled the flight before midnight.

Now that that was over I could concentrate on my future as a cricketer once more. I knew I'd have to make up my mind where I was going by the end of the month. Come September there would be all sorts of player movement and I might miss the boat. All the various possibilities were affecting my state of mind. There was an emotional thing going on too, because here I was preparing to leave a place that had been my second home from childhood. I knew I would find it difficult to concentrate on the field, so I had a talk with Neal Abberley. We agreed that there was little point in my continuing to play even second XI cricket now.

By this time there was interest in me from all over the place: Derbyshire, Kent, Hampshire, Durham... I was juggling far too many options. The family were all pressing me to go to Worcestershire, but I knew that whatever I decided, my Mum would back me all the way. It might hurt her to see me go to the other end of the country, but she was stoic, and had a firm belief that if I followed my heart's desire it would all work out for the best – except as far as potential wives were concerned. At the same time, however, some of the more respected members of my community called at the house to talk things through. They could remember the days when I played in the street and was allowed to score runs because I was such a weedy little kid and could hardly hold a bat. They were proud of what I'd achieved and didn't like the idea of me going so far away. They tried to persuade me to take up Worcestershire's offer. In a way they were saying I owed them something, but I wasn't sure that it amounted to that kind of loyalty. It felt to me as if they thought they owned a part of me.

To help me see through the fog I went down to Redruth in Cornwall to see my old PE teacher and mentor, Pete Bolland. He'd moved down there, remarried, and was raising a family. I trusted Bollo. He knew my game inside out. I told him I wanted this move to be the only one of my career. I didn't want to be one of these players who does the rounds and never really settles anywhere. Pete got me to go through the advantages and disadvantages of each county, and that way we narrowed it down to a straight choice: Worcestershire or Sussex.

When Tony Pigott persuaded me to visit him in Sussex to have further talks I went down early and had a look around Brighton. It struck me as a really laid-back place, with all the attractive cafes and bars that it was famous for. It would be good to be by the sea, too: healthier than Small Heath. As for the ground at Hove, I'd always enjoyed playing there. The first thing that struck me was the difference in atmosphere around a small club like that as opposed to a Test county like Warwickshire. It was a homely little ground – although I didn't realise that part of the homeliness would extend to us players having to paint the dressing-rooms pre-season! But then you could say that that was part of the team bonding. Warwickshire would fly us out to southern Africa – if selected; some lesser counties would take the guys paint-balling or rock-climbing; we were given a paint-brush and a pair of overalls each and told to get on with it.

I looked around the place, met Ruby the tea-lady – and sampled her famous rice pudding – and then listened as Tony sold the club hard, telling me he wanted me to return to Birmingham that evening a Sussex player. We agreed terms after a little negotiation. There was no agent involved; the paperwork was drawn up, and I left that night having signed on the dotted line. I would be on £25,000 a season, a nice £5,000 rise on what Warwickshire were paying me.

On the way back home I called my friends and family and told them the news. Next morning I drove over to Edgbaston to see the boys. It seemed that everyone there was happy for me, genuinely so. I went and found Phil and Neal Abberley to thank them for everything they'd done for me over the years. It was an emotional moment, and the thought of finally leaving behind the

CHAPTER 16 : WARWICKSHIRE: THE END OF AN ERA

friend-ships, the banter, the camaraderie of that dressing-room almost choked me. But I refused to let it. I only allowed myself to feel the relief of having my immediate future sorted out. The pain and the sadness, well, that would have to come later. I was leaving behind me the memories of a bizarre final season: two games for the firsts, and barely 50 runs; 13 for the seconds in which I'd been top scorer with 1,158 runs at an average of 55. It didn't make sense.

I collected my gear from the dressing-room on a non-playing day. It was deliberate. There were too many people I'd rather not see, the way I was feeling. But Trev Penney and Dom Ostler were there picking up some washing, as was Keith Piper. It all seemed so normal, except that they would be back next day, and I wouldn't. We kept it all light-hearted. Congrats on your new contract, mate. Yeah, Sussex eh? Good luck. See you around.

A day or two later, I was at home when Nadeem Shahid phoned me. It's a small world, county cricket. I knew him from games against Essex seconds, but he had since moved on to Surrey and had a place in Fulham. He'd heard I was on the move and invited me down to visit him. He was one of a number of friends I now had among the Asian contingent in English cricket – including Raj

Rao at my new county. We had formed a sort of loose-knit community within cricketing circles, and knew we could express our worries to each other since we all shared the same insecurities. It was good to see so many breaking through, guys like Aftab. Habib who'd left Middlesex and made the grade at Leicester, Usman Afzal who'd fought his way into the Nottinghamshire side, and Kabir Ali at Worcestershire. None of them had found it easy.

When I went down south Nadeem introduced me to a few of the Surrey lads – Adam Hollioake, Ed Giddins and Ian Salisbury. There were a few raised eyebrows at the news I was off to Sussex. Ian Salisbury sent a shiver down my spine when he said, 'Well, good luck mate; rather you than me.' However, I wasn't going to let that sort of thing get me down. There was a wind of change blowing through the south coast outfit, and I would be part of it.

In October I was invited down to Hove for an evening with the members, and to meet the boys. Normally around the county circuit you get to know players from most of the other clubs, but I'd never really met this lot. Chris Adams, aka Grizzly, had just arrived from Derbyshire, and Michael Bevan from Australia, so there was a real sense of this being a new era for the club. I was

CHAPTER 16 : WARWICKSHIRE: THE END OF AN ERA

interested to see what the players and staff were really made of. At Warwickshire we'd had a winning habit and a winner's mentality. Sussex had been on a long losing streak. How would that affect them, and what effect would the influx of new players, myself included, have on the side?

For a start, the average age was a lot younger than what I'd been used to. Peter Moores was a new appointment as coach, although he'd been with the club some years as wicketkeeper. He was in his late thirties. In my mind, of course, Sussex was always associated with the legendary Imran Khan, who had played for them through the eighties. Dermot, who'd been at Sussex before moving up to Edgbaston, used to keep us entertained for hours with his Imran stories. He had a flat overlooking the ground and at one stage, when he was suffering from shin-splints, the guys would look up from deep fine leg and see him lounging on his balcony in his regal splendour with yet another beauty – allegedly Stephanie Beauchamp was one of a string of females he entertained up there – bringing him a late breakfast in her night-gown. The talk was that once he had conquered Brighton he moved up to town and started on the Sloanies. Imran was a huge personality with a massive presence, not to say a legendary cricketer. Paul Smith once told me that when he was batting for Warwickshire he was greeted by Imran, following through and eyeballing him from about eight yards. 'Smith,' he said, 'I'm going to kill you!'

Now that the move was settled, I went back to thinking about my game. I'd been going to see Steve Bull, a sports psychologist of some renown who worked with the England hockey and cricket teams. I had seen the change in Nick Knight's game when he'd had a few sessions with Steve at Edgbaston. He was far more channelled, he had a well worked out pre-match routine, and he seemed far more single-minded. In addition, his form improved markedly. Seeing this made me wonder whether the magic could work for me. As a teenager I'd displayed lots of flair, but that had been stifled by the need to justify my presence in the side. At first I imagined I'd be lying on a couch telling Steve about my dreams or my childhood or something, but really our sessions amounted to intense discussions where he gave me mental exercises to do as well as analysing the state of mind I was in. Among other things he taught me to 'control the controllables' – in other words to accept that there were some things in life we could do nothing about.

Until I'd found a place to live in Brighton I continued to practise at Warwickshire.

CHAPTER 16 : WARWICKSHIRE: THE END OF AN ERA

There was no problem with that. I now had a good personal relationship with Neal Abberley: he had mellowed over the years and wrote a warm tribute to me in the county's yearbook, stressing my professionalism. After Christmas I went down south and had a talk with Keith Greenfield, who was coaching the seconds at my new county. I told him this was to be my first time away from home, apart from the winters Down Under of course, and he advised me to buy a place in Brighton rather than rent. As was normal, the club had agreed to pay for my first year's accommodation. So I now spent every other weekend in Brighton looking at flats. House prices were reasonable at the time, so it was a good time to buy. I got to know a friend of Tony Pigott's, an estate agent called Simon Caplin. He soon found me a nice little place within 10 minutes walk of the ground, a two-bedroom maisonette just off the sea-front. I moved in in February 1998 and soon had it furnished, thanks to my mate Rocky and his pine furniture factory, but with the season still a month or two away I felt pretty lonely most of the time. It wasn't like any home I'd ever known. So while I waited for the rest of the lads to gather for our first training sessions, I ended up driving back to Brum once a week, a nice round trip of 320 miles.

At Edgbaston, I now saw, I had been spoiled, with warm-weather training very much a part of the pre-season build-up. On three occasions they'd flown us out to Cape Town. At Hove they pulled the purse-strings a bit tighter: we stayed at the club and worked on our general fitness, then went to a nice holiday retreat in Aldershot – the army barracks, where we were put through a tough series of exercises designed to make men of us: running through freezing cold ditches, clambering up ropes and being shouted at. In Pete Moores we had a hyperactive leader who expected us all to do everything at the most intense level possible. If hard work really would reap benefits, well, the county's season promised to be better than the last one. Mooresy's approach caused me problems at first. I'm a player who's used to preparing hard, but then I like to relax. Mooresy seemed to think that if you weren't going hell for leather every minute you were slacking. I could see his point, which was to rid the club of what he saw as laziness – and, fair enough, he got results in the end. He just took a bit of getting used to.

Whereas at Edgbaston we used to intersperse all the usual dressing-room banter with some serious talk about cricket, this was missing at first at Sussex. Being a newly assembled team, there was no established pecking order, as it were. At the

CHAPTER 16 : WARWICKSHIRE: THE END OF AN ERA

beginning people were shy about chipping in – or worried that they'd come across as too big for their boots. Mooresy recognised that, and started to get the lads examining the finer points of the game. He tried to get everyone to contribute little phrases or mottoes that would gee us up. We were a bit embarrassed at first, but once we saw how corny his were – 'Do it', for example – we started chipping in.

Rather than coming up with corny slogans, I tried to put forward my opinions and advice, but immediately felt they weren't really welcome. It was all very difficult. Pete, and our captain, 'Grizzly' Adams, were trying to impose their own personalities on the team and I think there was a suspicion that everything I said was 'When I was at Warwickshire we used to do it this way...' Grizz, of course, had come from Derbyshire, where winning wasn't exactly a habit, and as a more than capable player he had strong views about how to change that. But apart from this slight tension I found Grizz pretty approachable at first. He definitely wanted to be one of the lads. Like most of the guys I ever played with, he had a healthy interest in beer. As far as I could see, it all looked set up to be a good season. We had a lot to be optimistic about.

CHAPTER 17

A new start at Hove

OUR FIRST Championship game of the new season was at home to Lancashire. I was in reasonable form, having batted okay in the friendlies without ever going on to make a big score. These pre-season fixtures are all about getting your rhythm right and spending time at the crease. I'd managed that, and felt ready to get down to the real thing now.

On the morning of the game I drove to the ground to find I had a message from Andy Moles wishing me all the best. That gave me a real boost, to think that my old teammates had taken the trouble to find out who we were playing and when. We won the toss and put Lancashire in. It was a good decision: we snapped up Atherton for nought and had them all out for 266. With the weather cold and wet, a fair bit of time had already been lost. We needed to crack on, and the first ball I received, short and wide from Peter Martin, I leaned back and cut to the boundary for four. It didn't last long. I was out for 10. It was all academic, really: with the weather dominating proceedings, we declared at 75

CHAPTER 17 : A NEW START AT HOVE

for 4. Lancs then made a sporting declaration at 68 for 0, leaving us to make 260.

It really helps when you have a specific target in mind. You know what you have to do. Despite my first innings failure I certainly wasn't down-hearted. Understandably, there was a tension in the dressing-room as we prepared to open the innings. Batsmen were fiddling unnecessarily with bits of kit, readjusting their pads and gloves, deliberating over which bat to use. Throughout the previous season Sussex had only managed a couple of victories, and here we were, first game, within shouting distance of what would be a great win against one of the strongest sides in the Championship. I went in to bat determined to play an anchor role, holding things together. It worked pretty well. By the time I was out for 40 we were only a hundred runs short of the target and it was left to Robin Martin-Jenkins (63) to see us through to a well deserved victory.

Normally we would have gone out and celebrated, but to be honest, the lads were a bit shell-shocked by what they'd achieved. I wouldn't say we had a quiet night in, but we were certainly quite thoughtful as we let the result sink in.

Our next fixture, against Essex, was a non-event for me. I managed to get a raging chest infection plus a fever and had to pull out on the morning of the game. It was frustrating, because I thought my form was looking promising and I was still eager to make an impression. As a new face in the side I knew I wouldn't be able to relax until I'd shown the rest of the boys what I was really capable of. Reputations count for nothing at a new club: you have to do it all over again from scratch if you're going to earn respect. As it was, Chris Adams set down his marker for the season, scoring two big tons.

By the time we travelled up to Trent Bridge to take on Nottinghamshire I was over my infection and feeling great, physically. But now, of course, I was starting to be aware of the pressure. Cricket is such an unforgiving game. For a batsman it's probably unique among sports in that you're only allowed one mistake. Who's to say that when you're out first ball you wouldn't have gone on to make a century? I wasn't out first ball at Trent Bridge in the first innings, but I might as well have been: I made a big fat nought, trying to leave one outside the off stump. Apart from running yourself out that's one of the most frustrating ways to be dismissed. There's nothing and nobody to blame but yourself – and your own poor judgement. As I walked back to the pavilion I glanced up at the balcony and saw the guys sitting there in silence. It's at times like

CHAPTER 17 : A NEW START AT HOVE

these that you need your mates' support, but these guys hardly knew me yet. I was angry enough with myself; what could I expect them to be feeling?

Despite the set-backs, however, I was sure it was only a matter of time before I kick-started my season. In the second innings we were chasing a small target for the win, 70-odd, so I wasn't going to make much of a score whatever happened. That made it all the more maddening when I went for a pull shot and gifted a catch to midwicket. As I stamped into the dressing-room the guys in there just carried on talking. There wasn't a lot they could say to cheer me up. I went into the shower area, shouting at the top of my voice and hurling my helmet against the wall. In the sudden silence I sat myself down. Once again I had got a start and not kicked on. Everyone else in the team had notched up at least one 50 and got their season under way, and there was I, the bright young prospect from the champion county, on a better contract than most of them could have hoped for. Looking back, I probably over-reacted. I'd made 27, and had actually top-scored as we stumbled to victory with four down, but my reaction was a measure of my desire to do well at a new club. I should have breezed through and carried my bat.

Back in Hove I spent some time talking about the way things were going with Tim Wright, our Australian physio. He assured me that the boys were right behind me. I realised I ought to be working on building up a good rapport with them. I was already getting closer to guys like left-arm opening bowler Jason Lewry and Raj Rao, a batsman who modelled his appearance on the rap singer Tupac Shakur. I was starting to relax in the evenings, and since a lot of the boys lived locally we now went out together regularly to places like Browns Bar in The Lanes, or the Beach Club on the sea-front. But it takes time to get to know a whole new group of players, and a lot of us had been strangers in April. As well as socialising with the lads, I had occasional visitors from Brum. Raheena came down with her new husband Talat and my nephew Hamza; my mate the ex-Aston Villa player Tony Morley showed up one weekend.

I now had a few days break before the next game, a Championship fixture against Derbyshire, at home. I put the time to good use, spending a lot of time with Mooresy, working on my technique. He was trying to get me to stand still at the crease, and generally relax a bit more. My problem was that I'd been letting my head drop towards the off-side. For the Derby game we were

CHAPTER 17 : A NEW START AT HOVE

minus Grizz. He would have loved to play against his former teammates – especially his old sparring-partner Dominic Cork – but he'd been called up for England's one – day game against South Africa, leaving Michael Bevan to take over the captaincy. Bev at this time was regarded by many as the best one-day player in the world. He played the game with a frightening intensity. He was deeply into body culture and fitness and you'd sometimes see him admiring his physique in the dressing-room mirrors. He wore speedos, like an Australian lifeguard, and one day I thought I'd amuse the boys by putting a pair on myself – over the top of my trousers. It had them rolling in the aisles – but I made damned sure I didn't let Bev see me, or I'd have been the one in stitches.

We were playing at Horsham, and as I drove away from the coast and through the Sussex Downs I tried to fill my head with as many positive thoughts and images as I could summon up. But when I got to the ground and had a net I found I was hitting the ball really badly. My timing was all wrong. Neil Taylor, one of the senior players, was standing behind me telling me that my back foot wasn't in line. He was trying to be helpful, but I remember thinking that on the morning of a game that wasn't the most constructive thing to say. I turned a deaf ear and concentrated on more positive thoughts, something I'd learned from Knighty and Steve Bull and had reinforced by the books I'd been reading. By the time we won the toss my timing still didn't appear to have improved, but it was too late to worry about it.

Horsham was a slow wicket, but true. If you got in on it there were runs to be made. Derbyshire had a pretty classy opening attack of Cork and Phil De Freitas, both of them England bowlers. After he'd sent down his first two deliveries, which came through nice and slow, Corky turned around to his players, hands on hips. 'Here we go boys,' he said, 'I see the captain's prepared a nice wicket for himself.' That was a dig at Michael Bevan, who had a bit of a reputation as someone who didn't relish batting on quick bouncy wickets – but then I've never met a batsman who does. Corky was just playing his usual mind games. He loved to get under your skin and sow the seeds of doubt, but he wouldn't get to me this morning: I was feeling better than I had any right to feel after that net. Why was that? I've no idea. Some days it just happens. Maybe the preparation had done the magic after all. Whatever the case, I was standing nice and still at the crease and moving late to the ball. Everything I did felt positive. Attacking or defending I was meeting the ball firmly; I was in the zone.

CHAPTER 17 : A NEW START AT HOVE

I looked around the tree-lined ground and there was Mooresy sitting on his own, egging me on to do well. With 40 minutes to go before lunch I'd passed 50, and was as confident as I've ever been of making a big score. But it wasn't to be. Shortly after the break I went for a big shot over the covers and was out, caught, for 70. As I walked off I felt a surge of relief. It wasn't the big one that had been there for the taking, but it was a solid enough innings. The boys were delighted for me.

We were all out for 325, and there followed a pretty torrid time in the field. Corky had been right in his assessment of the wicket, and was one of three centurions as Derby racked up 593. It was a long, long day and a half – made even longer after I made a couple of basic errors in the field, dropping one sitter and another slightly harder chance. So when we opened our second innings on day three, Michael Slater, their Australian batsman, called across to Phil De Freitas as he measured out his run, 'Don't forget, mate, he's got two catches to make up for before he even gets started.'

It was water off a duck's back. I was in superb nick and by close of play had cruised to 80 not out. All the time I'd spent with Mooresy working on keeping my head still was paying an early dividend. Sitting in the dressing-room winding down I knew I'd earned some respect from my new teammates as well. They'd heard about my reputation; now they'd seen what I could do with their own eyes. To my surprise I had a call from Dermot Reeve, who said he'd been following the score on Teletext. It just showed how complex people are. Dermot has been called self-centred, and worse, but here he was taking the trouble to congratulate a former teammate from 150 miles away.

If you're relaxed, it helps you play well, and if you play well it relaxes you. I was out till about two that night with Cookie and a couple of other lads, but I woke up next day feeling perfectly refreshed. When I got to the ground there were good luck messages from my Mum, and from a number of friends, including Pete Bolland. I was determined to convert my overnight 80 to a first century for my new county, so determined that I took the best part of an hour to get past the 90 mark. But I wasn't worried. I felt calm and assured, which probably explained why Corky pulled out all the tricks to unsettle me. As I stroked the ball past gully for four I was greeted with 'For fuck's sake, 10 years on and you still score all your runs down there.' I'd milked a lot of runs off him in that area when we first met up back in 1989 at under-19 level, and he'd never forgotten it.

CHAPTER 17 : A NEW START AT HOVE

I liked Corky. On his day he was a hell of a bowler, and he could bat when he put his mind to it. He got right in your face, but without the aggro he wouldn't have been half the player. It wasn't personal. It was his way of psyching himself up.

My hundred came up with a drive through extra cover off the spinner. There aren't many better feelings than hitting the ball off the meat of the bat and watching it split the field as it races towards the boundary. It was a fabulous way to bring up my hundred. I added another 25 before hitting one from Kim Barnitt straight down midwicket's throat. Even with 125 on the board it's a bit of a sickener to get out, but as I walked back to the pavilion I felt my Sussex career had really ignited. Grizzly was there to congratulate me. He'd finished the England one-dayers and had driven down to catch the rest of the day's play. 'Well done, mate. Let's make it a platform for the future.' With Michael Bevan scoring 127, we made 374, but that left Derbyshire with no more than 107 to make, and they polished them off fairly easily with the loss of three wickets. A good game for me, a lousy one for the team.

We were now due at Worcester for a Championship fixture and a one-dayer. In the four-day game Graeme Hick scored a pair of centuries to put Worcester in the box seat.

I'd been run out for 9 in our first innings, but made a tidy 50 not out in the second as we played out time for a draw. There was a one-dayer in among all this, and Mooresy told me to take the day off, so I went to visit my family in Birmingham. I spent the morning of the game sitting in my mum's back garden thinking about how things had changed. The previous evening I'd taken a look around the streets. The atmosphere was so different from when I was a youngster out there playing street cricket. Now there were far fewer kids, and there was a vaguely menacing atmosphere. Rather than a bunch of youngsters playing with a ball, there were knots of teenagers under the lamp-posts smoking spliff. And where we had spent the long evenings honing our skills with bat and ball, they had perfected the techniques of breaking into cars, nicking radios and flogging them for 15 or 20 quid in the next street. The trouble was that so many fathers now worked long hours to afford their families the things they wanted. Where were the authority figures to lead by example, or, when it was necessary, to instil a bit of fear into these kids? You couldn't blame the youngsters. They were just doing what we did when we were kids: pushing at the boundaries. Was it their fault that the structures simply gave way?

CHAPTER 17 : A NEW START AT HOVE

It was nice to be resting at Mum's house, but it made me realise that for all I needed to be away from home, I missed it. After a leisurely lunch I drove over to Worcester and ambled into the ground to see how the lads were getting on. It was decent day and I felt relaxed and quite perky. Mooresy, however, was frosty, to say the least. Why hadn't I turned up to practice? I'd thought it was optional, and said so. He didn't pursue it, but I realised that he was one of those coaches who think that a day off means a chance to practice, not a morning in the garden soaking up the sun. That's what he'd meant: get yourself down to the nets and do some work. At the same time I realised that his attitude only reflected his concern. He wasn't bullying me; he really wanted me to do well.

My form was okay over the next few weeks: not spectacular, but I never felt in trouble, scoring five fifties in eight innings. I shared a memorable stand with Grizz against Kent at Tunbridge Wells, the pair of us putting on 160 in about 30 overs to set up a 75-run win as the boys knocked Kent over twice for around 200. After that came a three-dayer against South Africa at Arundel, a picturesque ground set against the backdrop of the mediaeval castle. It's one of those places you really enjoy playing, the sort of ground where cricket ought to be played. In the South African party that year were two world-class bowlers in the shape of my old teammate Allan Donald and Shaun Pollock, who'd also spent a year at Warwickshire when I was there, plus Klusener and Kallis. It wasn't a bad line-up. But when we showed up on the morning of the game Bob Woolmer, now their coach, told us that the fearsome quartet wouldn't be playing. This was no surprise to us, as the fixture was sandwiched in between the first and second Tests.

South Africans play the game the way the Aussies do: they take it very seriously and play to win. They also like to indulge in the verbals. So it was no surprise to hear veteran spinner Pat Symcox welcome me and my opening partner with 'C'mon fellas, these blokes are playing for new contracts' – a bit of an exaggeration as we were barely into the middle of June. Brian McMillan was geeing their lads up as well. I was always told that he was one of the best – or worst – sledgers in the world, and it was almost a relief when he finally opened up at me. I was well settled, and had recovered from being bowled off a no-ball before I'd troubled the scorers, when I played at one outside the off stump and missed it by rather more than the proverbial coat of varnish. He pointed at the

CHAPTER 17 : A NEW START AT HOVE

Scoreboard and said, 'Hey pal, you're on 50 – at least try and look as though you know what's going on out here, hey?'

Despite the edgy stuff out in the middle, the South Africans were great off the field. At lunch, Symcox came over with a big smile and said, 'Well played young man.' AD greeted me with a big hug and wanted to get the latest gossip from the county circuit – and the lowdown on things at Sussex. It was nice too to catch up with Shaun Pollock. I liked the guy. I'd never really got to know him when he played for the Bears, even though I shared a room with him a couple of times, but I was struck by his deep Christian faith. You don't meet many pro cricketers who read the Bible every morning, and again at bedtime. He'd not had the best of times with us at Edgbaston. He'd started off in fantastic style with four wickets in four balls in a B&H match against Leicester, but then tailed off, succumbing to an ankle injury that cut his season short in mid-August.

The South Africa game was a bit of a damp squib after day one. We made 277, they replied with 96 for 0, and then the rain set in. It was a pity, because I would have liked to have renewed hostilities with the likes of Macmillan, Pollock, Symcox and the youngster Ntini. They brought the game alive.

Sussex were now developing nicely under Pete Moores. We were well placed in the table and the cares of the previous year were history. Slowly but surely the players were beginning to believe they could win games. Michael Bevan was a great influence in the dressing room, having that unquenchable Australian desire to win, and of course he had ideas of his own which he wasn't afraid to spell out. That caused a bit of a problem for Grizz as captain and Mooresy as coach, who were still trying to establish themselves. They were thick as thieves, but Bev was highly regarded by all us players. He could do it where it mattered: on the pitch. When he spoke, we all listened, which must have been difficult for Mooresy and Grizz as they tried to impose their ethos on the team.

Bev set himself very high standards, and expected no less from his teammates. If one incident summed him up it was the day I got myself run out against Somerset in a Sunday League game. It was my own fault: I'd slipped on a green pitch. When I got back to the dressing-room and Bev saw that I was wearing rubbers rather than spikes he let me have both barrels. 'You ever let me see ya wearing those again and I'll fucking kill ya!'

As a regular in the side I now found that successive matches were taking their toll.

CHAPTER 17 : A NEW START AT HOVE

The game against my old county at Hove was especially difficult. Part of me yearned to be mates with the guys, like I used to be; the other part of me knew I needed to be ultra-focussed and do well against them, that my own teammates would be expecting an extra effort on my part. Keith Piper told me later that the Warwickshire boys had decided not to talk to me on the field. Why make it easy? They preferred it if I felt awkward. And of course some of them chipped in with little comments – especially Ashley Giles, Trev Penney, the guys I'd been closest to. It was never malicious. Mostly they tried to make me laugh, which destroyed my concentration. When Ash called out in his best Neal Abberley accent, 'C'mon Waz, you want to get *holt* of it!' I cracked up. In the second innings there was no need for the jokes: Welchy got me for 5 as we slumped to an innings defeat.

After that my performances were, I have to say, patchy. For every decent knock there were two or three failures, but we were still putting the occasional win together and were to finish seventh in the Championship, a remarkable turnaround in the county's fortunes. The final game of the season was against Yorkshire at home. I made not very many in the first innings, and top-scored

with 49 in the second. To be honest I was glad it was now over. It had been a fair to middling season: one century and eight fifties, but when Tony Piggott called me in for my end-of-term review he offered me an extension to my contract.

CHAPTER 18

Grizzly times on the south coast

ALL I wanted now was to enjoy a couple of months away from the game before going out to Perth to prepare for another year. Back in the early nineties I'd met a guy in Western Australia called Peter Carlstein. Carly was a veteran South African who now lived out there. He was renowned for his superb coaching techniques and I knew that a couple of months with him – and a few games for my old club North Perth – would set me up for April.

It had been seven or eight years since I was in Perth, but when I showed up in the nets there was old Carly, his usual charming friendly self. 'Oh no,' he shouted to anyone within earshot, 'look what the cat's dragged in!' I strapped my pads on and walked into the net. 'Right, Wazzy, let's see if you've remembered a bloody thing I taught you, mate.' Carly was from a tough school. He believed you should be thoroughly prepared for whatever the opposition might throw at you out in the middle, so I had to get used to him calling me a shit Pom until it was water off a duck's back.

After he'd bowled me 10 or a dozen balls he walked down to my end. 'What the hell's happened to you, Wazzy? Where's the carefree boy I used to know? Where's the cocky little bastard who was never frightened to play his shots?'

This is why you need a change of scene, to get someone who'll take a fresh look at your game and see it with a clear eye. I knew I'd adapted the way I played but I hadn't realized how much I'd gone into my shell. Carly sat me down. 'Right, fill me in. What's been going on these last few years?' I didn't need to tell him that a lot of my natural self-confidence had gone, along with my flair, that my first aim was to survive early on in my innings rather than impose myself on the bowler. I was content to wait for things to happen rather than make them happen, passive rather than active. That's the way a lot of the older players will tell you to conduct yourself: play yourself in, wait for the bad ball, let the bowler make the mistakes, be patient, and above all... cut out the risky strokes. It was all about security, and the need to make the retained list at the end of the season.

Carly worked me long and hard for the eight weeks I was out there. I never

CHAPTER 18 : GRIZZLY TIMES ON THE SOUTH COAST

complained, never argued. I had the utmost respect for the guy, and I wasn't alone. Counties like Surrey and Worcester were regularly sending their players out there for him to toughen them up, and if it was good enough for them it was good enough for me.

As well as working hard with Carly I found time to socialise and catch up with a few old mates. Most of the guys I used to play with at North Perth were still there, so it was easy to fit in again. I generally soaked up the laid-back atmosphere, once again counting myself lucky to be so far away from the English winter as I went out running in the sunshine at 6.30 in the morning. By the time I returned home I felt fit and raring to go, with plenty of sound advice from Carly drilled into me.

Nothing Carly did could prepare me for what I found when I got back, however. After all that had gone into the previous year's turnaround in the club's fortunes, 1999 kicked off in dramatic style with massive upheavals at Hove. When Tony Pigott had arrived from Surrey he'd brought with him his mate, and former Surrey coach, Dave Gilbert. Dave had wanted to get away from the coaching side, it was understood, and had been appointed General Manager. Again, looking back, it's clear that Sussex was never going to be a big enough pond for the two of them, and when we reassembled for the new season Tony had been sent packing, and Dave was in charge of the playing side. Personally I was sad to see Tony go. I rang him and told him so, wishing him luck for the future. He was passionate about the club, he was Sussex through and through, and he'd learned a bitter lesson. I think he'd lost a friend too in Dave Gilbert. The last I heard of Tony he'd bought a pub and was also a pitch inspector for the ECB.

So now we had to get used to another head coach and another style, as well as a number of new players. The new signings included Tony Cottey from Glamorgan, Richard Montgomerie from Northants and Umer Rashid from Middlesex. Monty was an opening bat, a right-hander, which meant that my place – as well as my fellow opener Toby Peirce's – was under threat immediately. I'd had a better season than Toby the previous year, so I wasn't unduly worried about that. You expect competition. In any case, pre-season was looking good: I was hitting the ball well, and Grizz and Mooresy were talking to me about our prospects as if they really expected us to build on last year's progress. I was looking forward to partnering Monty at the top of the order. We'd batted together for Warwickshire at under-14 and under-16

CHAPTER 18 : GRIZZLY TIMES ON THE SOUTH COAST

levels before he went off to Northants where, by his own account, he'd had a bit of a rough ride.

Just as the previous year, our opening Championship fixture would be against Lancashire, but before that there was our annual pre-season game against Durham. I opened with Monty, scoring 20-odd in the first innings. This being a friendly, we were allowed to chop and change our line-up between innings so Toby partnered me in the second. I sort of envied the way he played. He was relaxed, knowing that it was just a warm-up and that he'd be sitting out the first competitive fixture in the seconds. He made a fluent 50 to my slightly tense 30 or so.

The day after the Durham match I was called into Mooresy's office. I'd played enough cricket to know that they weren't having me in so that they could wish me all the best for the new season. Sure enough, when I opened the door I saw Mooresy himself and Grizz sitting there. Grizz couldn't bring himself to look me in the face, and Mooresy was looking pretty uncomfortable. I closed the door. As the old saying goes, you don't need a. weatherman to tell you when it's raining. Before I even had time to sit down Mooresy had started.

'Look, mate, this is the hardest decision I've ever had to make but the fact of the matter is... it's been decided that we're going with Toby for the first game.'

My immediate reaction was to question how one innings in a practice game could turn everything around. I'd had a decent season last year; I'd demonstrated my commitment to the side; I'd gone out to Australia and worked hard; I was fit and seeing the ball well. All I needed now was a run of games to get me going.

I argued my case, something I would never have done in my Edgbaston days, but Grizz sat there with his head down. I tried to put a reasoned argument together, but they were having none of it. That's when I let rip at my captain. I told him straight.

'You're out of order, and you know it. All winter I've worked my rocks off over in Perth. I'm in great shape, and you know it. And now this. Why? Because Toby scored a few runs in a knockabout friendly?'

He had nothing to say. There was nothing he could say, and he knew he didn't have to respond. He was in charge, and he was going to have it his way. He could afford to let me have a little rant; then he could get on with his day. In the end there was nothing for me to do but leave, slamming the door behind me.

The boys didn't say anything. I made my feelings perfectly clear, and tried not slag

CHAPTER 18 : GRIZZLY TIMES ON THE SOUTH COAST

off Mooresy or Grizz. You have to think of your own dignity. Why let them turn me into the kind of person I wasn't? I've never thought of myself as vindictive. I try to accept what happens to me. But when the team was read out an hour later I could see from the look on the guys' faces that they were almost as shocked as I was.

I left my car at the ground and made the short walk to my flat. I thought about the home environment I'd left behind in Birmingham and suddenly Brighton didn't seem such a nice place after all. The trouble was I had no one left to be angry with. I'd certainly upset Grizz with my reaction, but as for Toby, who'd taken my place, well, it was hardly his fault. He'd be phoning all his friends and family and they'd be watching his progress on Teletext. They'd be delighted for him, and so they should be. But Grizz? He plainly didn't want me in his side, and I had no idea why not.

I'd been sitting at home for a while when the phone rang. It was Keith Greenfield, the second team coach, asking me to meet him – not at the ground but on the sea-front. There was a little cafe down there that was generally fairly quiet in the afternoon. Grubby, as he was affectionately known, was one of life's good guys. He knew what had happened and he felt for me.

He couldn't put things right there and then – nobody could – but he promised he'd help me in every way possible to fight my way back into the first team. He had been dropped a number of times in his career and knew what I was feeling. He came across quite simply as a decent guy and a friend, and I appreciated that. By the time we parted I felt a bit more upbeat. I went back to the flat, and started to unpack all the clothes I'd got together for the trip up north, then called my mother.

The great thing about having a mother is that you can unload on her, any time, and she'll listen. I told her exactly what had happened and how I was feeling. She needed to know everything, because back in Small Heath next day everyone would be reading the papers and calling at the house to ask her what was up, why wasn't I playing, and so on. Her door was always open, even when she was out visiting. She'll regularly call on eight or 10 people a day up and down the street and drink tea while they talk over what's happening. There are pluses and minuses with having a tight-knit community such as we were part of. You have no secrets, and you have to act out your life in public much of the time. Yes, you get the support, and that's great; and you get the plaudits when things go well, but when you

CHAPTER 18 : GRIZZLY TIMES ON THE SOUTH COAST

want space and time to lick your wounds in private, it's not always there. That was one reason why I preferred to live away at that time in my life.

After I'd spoken to Mum I got a call from Tony Cottey. Keep your head up, mate, and all that. Things'll turn around. I thought that was a great gesture from a guy who'd only arrived at the club from Glamorgan a few weeks before. When the chips are down you really find out what people are made of. I'd made it a point to do the same sort of thing the previous year when I was a regular and other guys were in and out of the team. I don't think you really know how valuable that sort of support is until you've been down that road yourself.

The next morning I had to turn up for practice with the second team. I may have been naively hopeful, but when I left Warwickshire I'd assumed that at 28 I was through with all that, but of course every season runs its course and your fortunes rise and fall just as they do in any other aspect of life. Grubby was as supportive as he could be, but it didn't alter two simple facts: one, I was back in the seconds; two, I would only get back into contention by making runs.

At the same time as worrying about myself I was now in the kind of position that everyone who has ever been dropped finds himself in, keeping an eye on the scores from Old Trafford to see how my replacement was doing. In a way I didn't want to know. Checking on Toby was a sure way of arousing the kinds of feelings I felt I should avoid: envy if he was doing well, some sort of guilty pleasure if he failed. But in the end you have to face these unpalatable truths, and when I did check the TV screen I found that he was still batting at lunch on the first morning. Seventy not out. As I read it it was as if a door was being shut firmly in my face. Decision justified.

I must have been harbouring more resentment than I realised. In the middle of a match at Maidstone against Kent seconds I got into a stupid slanging with Grubby over absolutely nothing. He hadn't done anything to deserve it, and I knew it. We'd had a long day in the field and he felt we hadn't really put our backs into it. He made us do a lap of the ground. When we got round as far as the pavilion he said, 'All right, let's go again.' To me it all seemed bloody pointless, and I said so. 'Just fucking do it,' he said. I sat myself down on the grass. 'To hell with it, there's no point,' I said. In the end of course I relented, but I realised I'd challenged him in front of the other players. It was inexcusable. It was out of character too. The fact was that I was

CHAPTER 18 : GRIZZLY TIMES ON THE SOUTH COAST

becoming increasingly bitter about my situation within the club and had started to lose respect for the people around me. It wasn't a good sign.

Amid all this unpleasantness I got a lot of support from Raj Rao. I rated him as a player, but he had had few real opportunities to get into the first team. He'd played for Middlesex before moving down to the coast. He was a decent middle order batsman and bowled some good leg-spin. Inwardly, I questioned his commitment to the game, and wasn't too surprised when he dropped out, going on to do very well for himself as a minor property tycoon. I was also pally with left-arm spinner Umer Rashid. Umms had a real swagger to the way he walked, on and off the field, a very talented all-rounder, and he became a great mate.

Now that I'd missed a series of first-team games all my friends, within the game and on the outside, were wanting to know what the hell was going on, and I had to tell them the truth: I'd fallen out with Grizz, big time, and I had no idea what was at the bottom of it. In my opinion he only really wanted to work with people who thought a lot of him and would massage his ego. That may be a harsh judgement, but it's what I felt at the time. I'd grown up at Edgbaston in an environment where everyone was supposed to express himself. There were no prima donnas up there, and no respect for mere reputation. You were deemed to be as good as your most recent stats, and that was all.

There was now a massive gulf between me and Grizz, not to mention an atmosphere. Whenever we crossed paths around the ground we kept words to a minimum, and in the end I was pretty sure he was avoiding me. The fact was that I had nothing pleasant to say to him, so I kept my mouth shut. Some time in May Toby scored his maiden first-class hundred. It wasn't looking good. Even so, I called the guy and congratulated him. He appreciated the gesture and said so, which left me wishing we could've been mates. He only lived at the back of my flat, a couple of minutes walk away. But that was never going to happen. We were both grasping for the same prize, and only one of us could have it.

From the outside the solution to my problem was simple: play yourself back into contention. For a batsman with any sort of claim to quality there are undoubtedly runs to be had in seconds cricket. The bowlers simply aren't as dangerous, nor the quality as sustained as you'd expect at county level. You get more loose balls. The trouble was that there were now fewer opportunities at

CHAPTER 18 : GRIZZLY TIMES ON THE SOUTH COAST

that level. In order to reduce costs over recent years, counties have cut back on their playing staff and sometimes struggle to get a second XI together. Around this time Sussex decided to reduce the number of second team games in order that players could have more quality time practising and working on their own. This was all well and good for established first-teamers who might welcome a 10-day break between games, but for someone in the position I was now, needing to put a string of scores together, it felt like another avenue of opportunity being blocked off.

By mid-July Monty was going from strength to strength in the first team. He'd followed up a half-century in the opening game with a hundred against Northants and could do no wrong. Toby, after his bright start, was struggling.

People who knew me were starting to question me again. If Toby was having a bad time wouldn't it make sense for me to be recalled? I tried to keep my feelings to myself, but mates like Umer would press me. Why was I out in the cold? Was something going on between me and Grizz? I wasn't spending so much time with Ums at that time, since he was now establishing himself in the first-team squad, but we remained quite close. He was a really engaging guy who had the support of a wonderful family. Obviously we had one thing in common, our racial background, and there was the fact that we'd made the effort to break out of the mould as it were. They were good for me, mates like Umms and Raj Rao, but I was finding it a strain answering the same questions over and over – not just from them but from other acquaintances. 'How come you aren't playing when Toby's lost his form?' What could I say? That the captain didn't like me? That would sound like sour grapes.

Deep down I really started to feel that my career was on the line here. I was drifting. I didn't know what I was supposed to do to get back in favour. When things went against me at Warwickshire I had managed to get my head down and keep churning out the runs. But I just didn't have the same determi-nation now. I was older. I'd proved myself, and maybe the concentrated effort over so many years had taken too much out of me. I decided to have it out with Grizz. I caught him at the back of the dressing-room one evening and asked him straight. 'Look, mate, is there a problem between you and me?' He looked me right in the eye. 'No, there's no problem, mate. Just keep it going.'

Keep it going: the same old refrain. I was sick of it. I'd heard it so many times at

CHAPTER 18 : GRIZZLY TIMES ON THE SOUTH COAST

Edgbaston. Grizz hadn't answered my question at all. If his words were meant to encourage me, they had failed. There was a blockage there, but I couldn't work out what it was. Now the only light on the horizon was the end of the season, barely six weeks away. I was doing something I never could have imagined, wishing the time away. It wasn't a healthy sign for someone who had dedicated his life to the game that was once his only passion.

I was sick at heart; that was the truth of it, and it affected me in all sorts of ways, finally undermining my professionalism. As a second-teamer I was expected to play local league cricket on a Saturday. It was compulsory. It could be fun, but I wasn't crazy about it: who needed another game at the weekend after four or five days of cricket midweek? The only time we were let off was after a seven-hour coach trip back from Durham one Friday night. Most of the boys felt the same as I did, and we all liked to have a little gripe about it. On the other hand, from the county's perspective, it was vital that they try to raise the standard of the leagues locally by having a few pros involved. It was their way of bridging the gap between club cricket and the county game. And as a batsman, if I played to my capacity there was the pleasure of scoring heavily against fairly modest bowling. All things considered, it was fair enough.

The biggest club in the Sussex League was Brighton and Hove. Raj Rao and Grubby played for them. My team was Littlehampton, a few miles to the west. Hugh Griffiths, the Sussex Secretary, had connections there and was keen for one or two of us to turn out for them and maybe help them to promotion from the First to the Premier Division of the Sussex League. They were a better-than-average outfit, although like a lot of clubs they had some pretty wacky characters in their line-up – like Disco, for example. Disco was a West Indian bowler of military-medium pace. When we were batting he'd patrol the edge of the playing area, blowing on a shrill whistle and waving his Trinidad flag. Every time we scored a boundary he'd give it an extra wave, do a little jig and shout things like, 'Someone call da police! Dere's a bowler gettin' murdered out there!'

The guys at Littlehampton were fantastic with me, always making me feel welcome, treating me like a star, but to be honest I was struggling to motivate myself. I didn't feel good about it, but there it was. One particular Friday, after I'd had a decent week in the seconds, and a couple of long days at the crease, I decided that the last

CHAPTER 18 : GRIZZLY TIMES ON THE SOUTH COAST

thing I needed was a second division league game next morning. I just wanted to chill. Of course, I should have called the club to explain that I wasn't available. I could've concocted a thigh strain, a stomach upset, anything. But I didn't. I knew it was wrong, but I just couldn't be bothered. It was a blistering hot day, and I spent it relaxing with some friends who knew nothing about cricket and could be counted on not to ask me about the internal politics of Sussex CCC.

I turned up at Hove on Monday morning feeling rested and refreshed. I went to the nets and everything seemed normal. The bowlers were firing in a few looseners at unguarded wickets and the batters were drifting across from the dressing-room, rehearsing their drives and cuts as they sauntered towards the nets. Grubby was chatting to the lads about how Saturday had gone in the leagues. Then he came over to me and asked me how I'd got on at Littlehampton. I wasn't going to lie. Hugh Griffiths would've been at the game and word would get back to Sussex soon enough. I told Grubby the truth. Right, he said. Come with me. He stormed off to the coach's office and I followed him, like a schoolboy in disgrace. Inside he let rip. What the hell did I think I was playing at? Didn't I realise I was letting the county down? How could I call myself a professional? I must admit I felt pretty small. What could I say in my defence?

Next day Grubby announced my punishment. I was fined £200 and would be suspended for the next game. I paid the fine, but after Grubby had had a chat with Mooresy the suspension was lifted. They needed me. I would travel up to Headingley for the game against Yorkshire seconds.

Just when I thought I was standing at the very edge of complete disintegration, out of the blue came a call from Mooresy. Monty had sustained an injury and I would be playing for the first team against Leicestershire at Arundel in a four-dayer. When Grubby had questioned my professionalism a few weeks earlier he had been right to do so. But now I knew it was never really in doubt. It was just lying dormant, awaiting the call. As soon as it came I could feel all the old adrenaline surge, the focus, the flow of energy through every part of my body – and not a trace of concern for the injured Monty. This was about me, and my future in the game I'd fallen in love with 20 years ago on the streets of Small Heath.

The day before the game I was training again with the first-team boys. I shuddered as I thought about the sheer humiliation of

CHAPTER 18 : GRIZZLY TIMES ON THE SOUTH COAST

my banishment to the seconds. I focussed hard, reminding myself that this was my big chance and I had to – absolutely had to – take it with both hands. Late that night I walked along the sea – front, alone in the dark, listening to the waves rattle the shingle. I felt calm, I felt composed, I felt ready.

Next morning I travelled the short distance to the beautiful old ground with Mark Robinson and Tony Cottey. They said it was good to have me back. It's just what I would've said to them if the circumstances had been reversed. I thanked them, but didn't have anything else to say. I had started to think about the Leicestershire attack: Chris Lewis, Alan Mullally, both former England players, and Mike Kasprowicz the Australian Test bowler. It was a quality line-up, but I had a good idea what they did with the ball, and I had my answers ready. I well remembered Mullally: it was he who'd got me out when I was playing for North Perth in the local derby against South Perth. As I met the other lads at the ground I felt fine; I couldn't wait to get started. There was a hum of chatter from the gathering crowd, and a warm breeze was drying any moisture off the square. I felt alive again. I deserved this, I kept telling myself. Come on.

We lost the toss, and Leicestershire batted. For five sessions and 160 overs spread over the best part of two days we laboured in the field as they piled up 566 for 8, with Aftab Habib batting for an age to score 166. Although it gave us a mountain to climb, I was glad for Aftab. I remembered him turning out for Middlesex seconds when he was only 16 and looking as though he was destined for big things. But he ended up playing way too much second XI stuff right into his early to mid-twenties. In the end he moved to Leicestershire, continued to apply himself and ended up being picked for the England Test side.

We had a stiff task on – no doubt about that – and were about to face an attack that had had the best part of two days to get themselves in the mood. Even so, as I walked out to bat after tea on the second day I felt positive. If their batsmen could rattle up a score like that on this pitch, why shouldn't I? I would get settled, then play my shots. The last thing I wanted was to scratch around. I would build my innings, not in tens, but in fives, ticking off the landmarks. Every run would count. If I say I treated this innings as if I were playing for my life it would be no great exaggeration. My first ball from Alan Mullally was perfect: shortish, and wide enough of the off stump to give me room. I stepped back and leathered it to the boundary, then allowed myself the luxury of a silent celebration. Yes, Wasim is back, and you guys had better believe it. Then back to my crease to concentrate hard, tapping my bat in the blockhole. New ball, new start.

My 50 came up in 71 balls. Not bad for an opener. I was already seeing visions of a century for the come-back kid. Wickets were falling steadily at the other end, which in a way made my success all the sweeter. By close of play I'd reached 84 not out. At stumps I walked off to a generous round of applause. I couldn't help wishing we had another half-hour for me to get to three figures. Nothing could have stopped me, surely.

I was due to go out for dinner with some non-cricketing friends that evening, but I couldn't get my mind off the game. I wasn't the best company. I toyed with my food. At nine-thirty I made my excuses and called it a night. I just wasn't with them. I went home and got straight into bed, but I couldn't sleep. I kept trying to tell myself I had nothing to worry about. I'd made 80; everybody else had got out cheaply. Point made, surely? In any other circumstances, yes; but whereas for the rest of the guys this was just another game, for me it was crucial to my whole season, maybe even to my future in the game.

Next morning I rang the guys, Tony and Mark, and told them not to call round for me. I'd be driving myself in. Why? Because I'd done that when I got my first ton for Sussex at Horsham, so maybe...

As I walked out to bat with Robin Martin-Jenkins I glanced up at the Scoreboard. We were starting the day almost 400 behind, so our first target was to save the follow-on, which meant we required a mere 250 more runs. But why not? I was in good nick, and so was Robin. Tucker, as he is known, is a classy player with bags of ability. Even then he showed every sign of being able to turn himself into a genuine all-rounder. And he was a nice guy too, a real gentleman with a terrible sense of humour, which meant that despite his public school background we had one thing in common.

The second ball of the morning was in the slot, slightly over-pitched, and I drove it for four. Eighty-eight. Next over Matthew Brimson came on, a left-arm spinner. Tucker pushed him into the vacant legside area for an easy single and we crossed at a leisurely pace, although I could hardly wait to get down the other end. This was going to be a stroll in the park.

All I remember about what happened next was getting a shortish ball. I went back to force it on the leg side, and whacked it into

CHAPTER 18 : GRIZZLY TIMES ON THE SOUTH COAST

short leg's midriff. He had no time to turn his back. He just grabbed at the ball as it popped off his stomach, and it stuck.

Of course I was unhappy, but on reflection, as I walked towards the pavilion, I realised I had put up a decent score and shown everyone it was a bit early to be writing me off. Back in the dressing-room I started to think about my whole approach to the game. Maybe this was what I needed in order to produce my best form. Pressure. Was I a bit too relaxed when the tension eased? Was that my problem? But more than any of these considerations, I felt relief flooding through my body. Surely now I'd get a run in the team. Grizz came in and said a brief 'well done', but that was about it. There was still an atmosphere between us, but I felt sure he was pleased with the way things had gone – even though it looked as though we'd be following on.

It might seem odd that I could follow a series of indifferent performances in the seconds with a good score in the first XI, but I'd put that down to the general level of intensity in the higher grade. It forces you to concentrate that much harder, to watch every ball, treat every bowler with respect. Look at the Test players, especially on tour, how poorly they often perform in the warm-up games before coming good when it matters, in the Tests. In short, it's a matter of taking the game seriously. In the seconds, it's all too easy to get a bit slap-dash. There's so much less at stake. At this level, everything and everybody around you – players, coaching staff, even the groundsmen and the facilities – reeks of professionalism. Going out to do your work in a top county ground is like going through a set of doors into a church, or a court-house or an art gallery. You feel a great weight of history, class, atmosphere, tradition. On a good day it's almost a spiritual experience.

The rest of the match went the way we knew it would, deep down. I made a modest 16 as we were bowled out for 214 to give Leicestershire an innings victory. We packed up and went our separate ways to prepare for a trip up north to face Derbyshire and Corky. We all went up a day early so that we could have a good practice session together. That went well, and I was feeling in good nick, but when I got back to our hotel late in the afternoon I found a message for me to call Raheena. That wasn't like her. It could only be bad news. When I got through to her she was obviously distressed. A close relative of ours had passed away, an uncle. There was no question of my not going home immediately, so I got in the car and drove through the rush-hour traffic to Birmingham.

CHAPTER 18 : GRIZZLY TIMES ON THE SOUTH COAST

Mum was in tears when I got to the house, and my sister did her best to comfort her as we headed back across town to our relatives' house. There were close to a hundred people gathered there to mourn, to offer their condolences, to see if their assistance was needed, and to pay their respects. It wasn't the most comfortable evening, as I sat with my aunts, uncles, cousins and friends of the family. It was a strange experience for me, not because I wasn't used to them all – I was – but this was the first time in years I'd been around the extended family and nobody had wanted to talk cricket.

By the time I'd dropped Mum at home and set off for Derby it was one o'clock in the morning. I got to my hotel an hour later. It wasn't ideal preparation for the day ahead, but I had no alternative. Neither did I resent it. I had been doing my duty as head of the household, the role I had assumed when my father died. It was both a responsibility and an honour.

In any case, I didn't feel too bad in the morning. A little tired, maybe, but I knew I had to get on with it. Monty was back in the side, partnering Toby, and I had been put down to number three. I'd batted there a couple of times for Warwickshire, but I'd never really got used to it. As an opener you know precisely how it goes. You win the toss, you pad up and out you go. No waiting around, no sweating on the fall of a wicket. No 'will it be five minutes or five hours?' You get in there and do your stuff. As a number three I hadn't the faintest idea whether to sit and relax, stay loosened up, or stand there as if I expected a wicket to fall next ball. Worse than that was sitting there and watching the ball do things, through the air or off the pitch, and seeing your guys struggling. You just start fretting about what you'll face when you get out there. No, I'd always settle for opening. There's less time to get into a sweat, less chance for your confidence to be eroded by the constant appeals, the oohs and aahs from the spectators as the ball whistles by the batsmen's heads.

As Monty and Toby set about building us a platform, I tried unsuccessfully to get the previous night's events out of my mind. Then, on the field, Corky struck, dismissing Monty cheaply. Out in the middle, I took guard and tried to recall all the pictures and sounds from Horsham the previous year when I'd scored 200 runs against this lot. It didn't work. Corky came in, pitched his first ball up to me and I shuffled across my crease. By the time I'd completed the move the ball had swung in and I was looking up for the dreaded

CHAPTER 18 : GRIZZLY TIMES ON THE SOUTH COAST

umpire's finger. 'That's out,' he said, and a gleeful Corky was doing his war-dance.

LBW. I was no stranger to that sort of dismissal. I'd like to have been, but I wasn't. I'd got out that way a number of times in my career, usually when I wasn't fully switched on, not 100 percent balanced in my stance and falling forward. I trudged off, gutted, but not exactly astonished. Back in the pavilion, I couldn't be bothered to do what I'd normally do, sit down and try to work out how it had happened and what I should do in future. I knew what the real problem was. I simply wasn't in the right frame of mind.

That evening I went back to Small Heath, hoping to relax and regroup. In hindsight it wasn't the brightest thing to do. The family were now all round at my mother's, everyone focussed on the loss of our uncle. People were crying, people were comforting each other, people were remembering. I would rather have been on my own, but my conscience was telling me I needed to be there. My mother wanted me and Raheena to stay with her, so I slept in my old room upstairs, slipping away next morning at about seven o'clock.

We'd been all out just before stumps the previous day, so with a day's fielding in prospect I felt fairly relaxed. Here was a chance to get my mind straight in preparation for our second knock, and to absorb the team atmosphere, dispel the mood I'd brought with me from home by enjoying a bit of banter with the guys. We bowled and fielded well, getting them out an hour before the close. As Toby and Monty prepared to open the batting I got into my own head, visualising six or seven different ways I could get off the mark if I had to bat tonight. This was something I'd learned from all those books Belly had made me read, and my sessions with Steve Bull. But even as I marshalled my thoughts Monty was out, leaving me about 25 minutes till close of play.

Sometimes you have this feeling of dread. You just know it isn't going to work out. And I knew, deep down, that this was one of those times, even as I walked across the square and had a quick word with Toby. All he said was, 'They're a bit lively, mate.' He wasn't wrong. The first ball from Phil De Freitas thudded into my pad and I knew the outcome without even looking up.

This was the first king pair of my entire career, and it didn't feel good. In fact it felt like shit. I tried to pick myself up by remembering what Andy Moles once told me, that you're not a real opener until you've chalked up a king pair. Scant consolation. Years later it becomes a nice

CHAPTER 18 : GRIZZLY TIMES ON THE SOUTH COAST

story, almost a badge of honour. Remember that time when…? But when it's just happened it simply hurts like hell. And the fact that we won a low-scoring game by 85 runs? That didn't seem to matter a great deal.

As I turned into Somerville Road that night I was still nursing the pain and thinking over my performance. Yes, I suppose I could excuse it on the grounds that I was distracted by family matters. But then I started to wonder whether I'd been feeling so good after the Leicestershire game that I'd gone up to Derby feeling complacent. I was determined to put things right now, and the chance came in a three-day game against an MCC side of young cricketers at Chichester. I scored an undefeated 214, and was pleasantly surprised when Grizz called to congratulate me. That was the first really civil exchange we'd had since the bust-up.

Despite these encouraging signs, however, I had to wait four more weeks to get back into the first XI, and even that was only because Michael Bevan was flying out to Australia, having been selected for their one-day squad.

Fate has many twists, and here was another one: my return would be against my old county, at my old home ground. It would be a special moment, one that the press had already picked up on. A couple of days before the game a reporter from Birmingham called and asked me how I felt about my return. I can't remember what I told him, but I remember the headline we read when we picked up the *Birmingham Post* the day before the game. Wasim, it seemed, was 'out to end Warwickshire's season.' So I was opening against my old county on the back of a king pair at Derby and with all my old mates having read that I was out to 'do' them. They would be loving that.

There was no dream return. It was a total disaster. We were skittled out for 99 and 176; Warwickshire's 207 – with a young schoolboy named Ian Bell making a duck – left them a second innings target of 70-odd, and we were comprehensively beaten. I tried to put on a brave face. Things would come right. They were bound to. Not for the first time I wished I was a bowler. Until the last wicket has fallen a bowler can always have one more shot, always has a hope that he can turn things around. Just one good ball, one stroke of luck, and you're suddenly firing again. When you fail as a batsman, that's it. No next ball to redeem yourself; you're back in the dressing-room with maybe a week to go until your next innings. If selected.

CHAPTER 19

12th man with a twist

IT WAS at this time, I am pretty sure, that Grizz made his mind up, rightly or wrongly, that I just wasn't right for Sussex. Towards the end of the season, as usual, the contracts meetings were scheduled. This is where they basically sat you down and told you whether you were in or out. When I walked into the committee room, past all the photos of Ted Dexter and Maurice Tate, John Snow and the Reverend David Sheppard, I wasn't sure what to expect. Looking at Grizz, Mooresy and Grubby – the firing squad as we called them – all sitting there at the long table, I realised I probably had a majority decision against me already. I knew I hadn't done myself justice, and of course I'd had that run – in with Grubby, not to mention the ongoing difficulty with Grizz. The other thought going through my head was that I was on a better contract than most of the guys. So long as I was playing so much two's cricket I was an expensive luxury.

Mooresy kicked things off by telling me that he felt I needed to play regularly rather than being in and out of the side. I thought that was a pretty bloody obvious thing to say, but I kept my mouth shut. 'So,' he continued, 'if you want to move on we won't stand in your way.' I felt a shiver of fear run through me. I hadn't realised I was that close to being shown the door. Then my natural defiance returned. I'd never quit yet and I wasn't planning on quitting now thankyou very much. What I could've said, but didn't, was that I'd been stuffed at the start of the season and they damned well knew it. They'd picked Toby ahead of me right through the season and what had he done? After a bright start he'd averaged 20. In the end I just told them that I wanted to fight for my place. I wouldn't give up. No way.

'Mate, that's music to my ears,' Mooresy said. I think he always believed in me, right to the end. The other two said nothing. As I left the room I was thinking what I've always thought. Next year was going to be the year. An incurable optimist, that's me.

At first my optimism seemed well founded. At the end-of-season party Grizz came over to me, put an arm round my shoulders and said, 'Mate, you'll be starting next season.' I remember that moment so vividly – partly because he was promising me what I would almost sell my soul for, but

CHAPTER 19 : 12TH MAN WITH A TWIST

partly because even as he said the words I found myself wondering whether I could really trust the guy. He'd persisted with Toby throughout the season and the guy hadn't exactly lit the place up. And what he was saying was a rash thing for anyone to come out with at the end of September. A lot of things could happen between then and April. I sort of wished he hadn't said it, yet of course I clung to the memory as a sort of security blanket. I would start. I would. It seemed to be the proverbial light at the end of a long dark tunnel, and nobody was there to remind me that sometimes that light is an express train heading towards you.

With the season over I got together with a couple of the boys, Michael Strong and Justin Bates, and decided that a holiday in the sun was what we needed. We flew out to Tenerife to soothe away the season's aches and bruises and damaged pride... but somewhere along the way I must've run over a black cat. I managed to fall off a banana boat and injure myself twice over, tearing the ligaments in my knee and a muscle in my hip.

Back home I went straight into hospital to have the knee operated on, and by mid-December it had completely healed up. No problem there. The hip, on the other hand, refused to get better. The club were fully aware of the situation, of course, but when I spoke to Mooresy about it he told me he'd had a word with Dave Gilbert. Their opinion was I should just grit my teeth and play through the pain barrier. All the same, in January I went to see a top hip specialist in Cambridge. Even as I made the journey I received a call from Dave. He needed me to be fit for the new season, and he wanted to know what I was up to. He knew as well as I did that if I had an op I'd be unlikely to make a full recovery this side of April. Reading between the lines I could only imagine that the club didn't want to be saddled with a big medical bill. They'd rather I got through the season. Then, if I still needed treatment, well, my contract would be up and it would be no concern of theirs. Like everyone else, they had a business to run.

I didn't have much choice. In part my desire – my *need* to prove myself – counted for more than any discomfort I felt in my hip. I would train on. It was now the end of January and I had two months to get myself fit, mentally as well as physically.

I started a gruelling four-hours-a-day programme. I worked on my game, I did weights, and I ran. Day after day after day. By eight o'clock each night I would be off to bed, exhausted and in considerable pain. But you can get used to anything, and in the end the sheer discipline of a regime like that, and actually managing to accomplish the challenges you've set yourself, gives you the will to carry on. Besides, I was doing what I was good at: fighting for my future.

In the pre-season games Mooresy and Grubby both commented that they'd never seen me play so well. As well as following my own fitness regime during the winter, I'd talked to a number of opening bats who'd made a success of this specialist position, guys like Mark Benson, David Smith and Hugh Morris, all of them left-handers. I travelled long distances to talk to them, be with them, listen to their game plans. As I absorbed some of their advice about concentration and confidence-building and practised it in the indoor nets, I felt I was looking a different player. With the season about to start I was in no doubt where I stood, however. I may have been in the last chance saloon, but I was primed and ready for the shoot-out that was looming.

As the opening game of the 2000 season approached I had never been better prepared. As well as my physical regime I had developed a mind-set like the one I had had at the beginning of my breakthrough season, 1995. Just as I had back then, I'd put the woes of the previous season behind me and was feeling 100 percent confident in every aspect of my game. When we got together all the lads commented on how well I was looking. In practice games I was playing positively, looking sharp, and scoring runs. I was relaxed at the crease and, having worked hard over the winter at playing the ball as late as possible, was reaping the benefits.

A couple of days before the first game of the season I went out for an early dinner with some friends. It was a beautiful warm early evening so I decided to walk home along the seafront. I leant on the railings to watch the plump seagulls bobbing on the waves. The sun was still shining and everything felt good. Everything.

I'd only been home a few minutes when the phone rang.

'Hello?'

'Oh, hi Wasim.'

'Mooresy, mate. What's up?'

'Listen, we've – er, we've decided to go with Toby.'

The first thing that struck me was that it was Mooresy who'd called. Why the coach rather than the captain? Why not Grizz? And what about those fine words at the end of last season, that I'd be starting? Easy to say, but now that he'd gone back on a promise why couldn't he make the call himself?

Along with my rage and disappointment, all the old thoughts cascaded through my

CHAPTER 19 : 12TH MAN WITH A TWIST

mind. Was it just that my face didn't fit? Was Grizz trying to get his own back for our falling out last year? Was it that I was on twice the money that Toby was on? Did that make him the better long-term investment? Or was it worse than all that-could they see something that I couldn't, something that nobody would tell me, that I just wasn't up to scratch? Deep down, though, right at the centre, I was calm. I knew, as I'd always known, that the script for my ultimate destiny was already written. As I said before, I believe in Fate. But that doesn't mean you surrender to circumstance. I would continue to do all the right things; I would carry on doing my very best. I would do everything within my power to control what I could control, but when Fate took a hand I had to recognise that there would be nothing I could do about it.

The day after the phonecall from Mooresy I travelled up to Essex with the seconds for a one-dayer. I find it hard to believe it, looking back, but despite what had happened I travelled to Chelmsford in high spirits. I still felt hugely confident about my physical condition and my form, still looked forward to the thing I'd always loved, strapping on my pads, walking out into the middle and taking guard on a freshly mown pitch with the sun on my back and the smell of damp earth and crushed grass in my nostrils. My good feelings proved to be justified that day as I cruised to 107. And afterwards, as I drove home around the M25 and then south into the calm of the Sussex countryside, I kept waiting to get the call from Grizz, or Mooresy, or someone. Anyone. Well done, mate. We're keeping tabs on you. But it never came.

I now adopted a new mental strategy. I would forget all about the first team. If the call came, fine; if not, well, I was being paid to play cricket, wasn't I? There were a hundred kids out on the streets of Birmingham every night who would think I'd hit the big time. What would I have thought as an eight-year-old if someone had said that 20 years later I'd be getting a decent salary, free kit, and could play on manicured squares in leafy surroundings and drive a nice car back to my flat beside the sea? I had a lot to be glad about, and I would now concentrate on each day and try to enjoy it as best I could. I even started to take pleasure in my weekend club cricket again. In 1999 I'd been offered the chance to play for Horsham. I'd always liked their ground, so I jumped at it, and had a good first season with them.

Leaving aside my exile from the first team, my game was in good shape. I felt good, I was balanced at the crease, and I was making runs. I knew that Toby was struggling in the firsts, but I tried to block that out of my mind and concentrate on my game, my form, my fitness. I couldn't control what he did, nor what decision Grizz might come to about selection. I made a point of not socialising with the first-team boys. You can't keep that up when you're out of favour. You feel like an intruder, as if you don't belong. When you're in the team, yes, it's a great feeling to be a part of that group. When you're out, you need to withdraw discreetly into the background. Besides all that, the last thing I wanted was to bump into Grizz. I was sure he was behind my being dropped.

Despite my upbeat mood, events on the field started to gnaw at my guts. I mean the first-team field, where Toby continued to struggle. Every time I saw Grizz I was half expecting him to give me some hint that my time had come. But nothing happened. I reminded myself that captains are bound to have players they rate and players they don't rate. It's human nature. He was maybe sticking with Toby because he believed in the guy, thought that he must come good.

By this time my friends and family were getting more agitated about the situation than I was. Tensions bubbled to the surface at Dom Ostler's wedding. I was invited, naturally, as was our old mate Rocky – and Grizz, who'd played club cricket with Dom out in Cape Town. Rocky couldn't resist having a go at Grizz for not sticking to his word and playing me at the start of the season. He felt very strongly about it. He was angry on my behalf. He reckoned Grizz was destroying my career, and was willing to say so. He told him he had no respect for him.

It seems strange looking back, but throughout the season, despite the way things were going, it never entered my head that I might leave Sussex. I liked my life down on the south coast. I had my flat there, which I'd now made comfortable, and I had my friends, within the game and on the outside. In just about every aspect of my life I was happy. It was just the cricket... Oddly, it was around this time that I had a rare bit of success as a bowler. I used to do a bit of medium-fast stuff in the nets, and once in a while I was asked to help out in a game. Against Surrey seconds at Sutton I took 5 for about 25, including a hat-trick. Maybe I'd been barking up the wrong tree throughout my career. I was prepared to believe anything by this stage.

As we got into July I became aware that we would shortly lose Michael Bevan to the Australian tourists for their one-day

CHAPTER 19 : 12TH MAN WITH A TWIST

matches. As far as I was concerned that offered fresh hope of a call-up to the first team. I had long since become resigned to the fact that Toby would never be dropped, no matter how badly he performed, but maybe there was a place for me at number three. My game was still good, although the runs weren't there at the moment. At the same time another player seemed to be in contention. Bas Zuiderent, who had already represented his native Holland, was younger than me and posed an obvious threat.

By now the Championship had gone to two divisions and we were pressing for promotion from the second. There were three games left, and I hoped that the selectors might think what I was thinking, that my experience might help us to edge it.

Even as I clutched at such faint hopes I found myself wondering what it had all come to. As a youngster, playing with great confidence and using the full range of shots without any fear, I had naively presumed that by the time I was 30 I would be in the England set-up, not hoping against hope that I could squeeze in a few games for a lesser county towards the end of a moderate season in the County Championship's second division.

But July gave way to August, Bev was due to depart the following week, and still there was no call. When I was younger I would have focussed my mind entirely on a positive outcome. Now, however, I had had enough experience to start preparing myself for the worst. Then, out of the blue, Grubby came up to me after practice one day. 'Mate, you're playing next week. Mooresy told me to tell you.' It seemed strange that the coach hadn't told me himself, or called me, but I didn't have time to worry about that. Here at last was the chance I'd been waiting for to resurrect my career.

Next day I joined the first teamers at practice. We always had a day together before we travelled. We were playing at Northampton, a ground I'd always done well at. Grizzly came over and had a word with me. 'Good luck tomorrow, mate.' Yeah, sure. I'd almost forgotten what they guy looked like. Next day I travelled with Nick Wilton, our wicketkeeper, in the team van. It usually fell to one of the younger players to drive the kit van and I was happy to keep him company.

At the hotel that evening I got a real boost when Mooresy came up, put his arm round me and said, 'Waz, you need to just go out and enjoy yourself tomorrow. There's absolutely no pressure on you, mate. All the boys know how good you are. Relax and express yourself.' It was just what I needed.

CHAPTER 19 : 12TH MAN WITH A TWIST

I'd already decided that this one would be for me. I would go into my bubble and play like I knew I could.

On the way up I got a call from Paul Bolton, my mate at the *Birmingham Post*. He was covering the game for one of the papers, was staying at the same hotel as us and wanted to meet me for breakfast next morning. It was good to see him again, and we had quite a chat before I went away to prepare for the game. He understood the position I was in and when he wished me luck I knew he meant it.

At the ground we won the toss and batted. As Monty and Toby strode out to the crease I sat with my pads on, anxious to get out there and get on with it. Since the disaster of my king pair at the end of last season I'd read a very helpful book called *Feel The Fear And Do It Anyway*. If I'd learned one thing from that book it was that fear was natural, often unavoidable, frequently necessary, and could be made to work for you. It needed to be channelled and turned into a positive force. That's what I was doing in my mind as I pondered the outcome of my comeback, and perhaps my fate as a professional cricketer, that August day. But I didn't have too long to sit thinking. Monty soon got himself out leg before. I would now be partnering the guy who had kept me out of the team for a year or more. As I walked out to the middle, my veins throbbed to the flow of adrenaline, while my body felt a deep calm. I prayed briefly. It was in God's hands now. I would do my best, but He would have His way. What do they say? Man proposes, God disposes. Whoever wrote that had it about right. Before I received the first ball I looked up at the press box, and saw Bolters give me the thumbs-up.

I let the first couple of balls fly by my off-stump, well wide. The third was slightly over-pitched, nicely in line, and I drove it through point for four. Even as it bobbled over the boundary rope I glanced up at the balcony where the boys were all sitting. I hoped they were feeling some of what I felt, which was relief, floods of it. Now I started to play like I knew Wasim Khan could play, fluently, confidently, and with style. In among all the feelings there was an element of defiance. Who the hell were they to drop me when I could play like this? I knew where that defiance came from. It came from way back when we were kids and we'd all talked about how the odds were stacked against us, and how we would battle through against the establishment and make the grade, all of us – especially my poor mate Parvaz, who was on the brink of making it

CHAPTER 19 : 12TH MAN WITH A TWIST

when his life was snatched away. We'd needed that fire in our bellies then, and it seemed I still needed it now. It felt justified, and it felt healthy. If it was anger, well okay – it was a righteous anger.

At the other end, wickets were falling regularly. It was a turner and in Jason Brown and Darren Cousins Northants had two bowlers who knew how to exploit it. But it was a challenge, and I was enjoying every minute of it. You don't like to see a succession of partners walking back to the pavilion, but when you do at least you have the satisfaction of having kept your end intact. After lunch Grizz joined me, but only managed to scrape into double figures before losing his wicket. On his day he could be one of the most destructive batsmen you'll see, but this wasn't his day. He was soon gone, and my new partner was Tucker Martin-Jenkins. He was always great to bat with. He offered you fantastic support out in the middle. 'Go on, Waz. Show them. Show them just what a good player you are.' At tea, as we sat having a drink, Grizz came over. 'Keep it going, Waz,' he said. He sat down next to me. 'Get yourself a big one, mate. Come on, you gotta get yourself a big one.'

I lasted about one over after tea, before being caught at silly point off a spinner for 74. It would've been nice to score a hundred, but the fact is I had put in a decent performance on a turning wicket and held things together, as we stumbled our way to a total of 232. It can't have been the pitch that did us. Northants rattled up 460 on the same track, and then had us out for 211 to win by an innings, my contribution being 14.

The season had about four weeks to run. I knew my game was in good shape, and I looked forward to reaping the benefits of my hard work with a decent run in the first team. After the Northants game it was good to pick up *The Argus,* and read a piece by Bolters under the headline 'He Khan Still Cut It.' It was a real confidence booster as we prepared for a return fixture against Northants at Eastbourne. Not only did he praise my batting, but pointed out that I was worth a new contract. Failing that, he said, I'd certainly put myself in the shop window for anyone wanting an experienced top-order batsman. It was like having a free ad.

The day before the game the news came through that Toby was being released at the end of the season. The fact is that he would probably have quit the game anyway since he had other interests outside cricket. I couldn't help feeling a slightly bitter taste in my mouth as I pondered the news. After all that his presence in the side had meant to me personally, he could afford to shrug

CHAPTER 19 : 12TH MAN WITH A TWIST

off failure and walk away. He'd been given every opportunity to succeed, and he knew it. All I wanted was a fair shake.

On the first day at Eastbourne the ball swung around as if it were possessed and we skittled the opposition out for out for 110. When we batted, however, we fared little better, gaining a slender 43-run lead. Their second innings total of 270 left us an improbable target of 313. Like us, Northants were pushing for promotion, so there was a lot at stake. They hammered home their advantage to wrap up a solid victory in just over two days. There would normally be no shame in failing to reach over 300 in the final innings, but we managed to bat abysmally, scraping our way to 65. It was a bitter disappointment for us, as well as for the sponsors of the Eastbourne festival. Although the pitch there wasn't up to much, having deteriorated over the years, a lot of effort went into providing hospitality in the tents and marketing the games there as a good day out for cricket-lovers and anyone else who fancied a trip to the seaside with some decent food and drink. It's a big let-down for the sponsors when the game is effectively over in two days – even if there was still a Sunday game to come.

After that shambles of a second innings the club felt it was a good time to have a meeting, right there in one of the marquees, and discuss contracts. We didn't know what was going on at first. We thought that Dave Gilbert, Mooresy and the others were talking about the side for the next match, although someone said that our Chief Exec Don Trangmar had joined Grizz at the meeting. It seemed to go on for a hell of a long time, and I suppose the alarm bells should have been ringing, given our abject performance on the field. We'd been out there playing touch rugby, and had come in for a shower. As Grizz and Mooresy came over everything seemed okay. I was told I was in the squad for Sunday's one-dayer, although Mooresy said it was unlikely I would play. That was okay. I was part of the set – up and it's normal to shuffle the pack for the limited overs stuff.

I spent Saturday relaxing with friends. Brighton was heaving with visitors, in town and along the seafront. You could see why teams liked coming down to play us at Hove: the place had a real buzz to it, and not a little glamour. In the evening I started to get my things together in preparation for next week's game against Glamorgan, even though we wouldn't be travelling till Monday. This time we were off to Colwyn Bay. They had a sort of mini festival up there in the summer to catch the North Wales holiday-

CHAPTER 19 : 12TH MAN WITH A TWIST

makers. As I drove along the coast towards Eastbourne on Sunday morning, I was looking forward to the trip. If the weather stayed as it was – it was a glorious morning with the temperature already in the high twenties and the sun shimmering on a calm sea – it'd be a great few days away. I was thinking how good it was to live down here compared with the crowded streets and fetid air of Birmingham on a hot summer's day.

When I got to the ground some of the boys were already about to have a net. I was in the dressing room getting myself organised, when Grizz came in. He said the usual hi, how are you doing, and went back out onto the field. When I came out I said hi to Mooresy and he asked to me to bowl at the batters in the nets. That was fine: it's what was expected when you weren't playing. I didn't mind. I enjoyed trying out different styles of bowling, imitating old-timers like Bob Willis or Jeff Thompson to amuse the guys. As we came off I asked Mooresy to hit me a few balls so that I could practise my catching. Even now when I think back I can't remember there being anything in the atmosphere whatsoever, no clue that anything out of the ordinary was about to happen. It was a routine morning's practice before a game. Afterwards I remember walking off with Mooresy, just pleased to be there, pleased to be a part of the whole set – up, back with the boys again.

Jason Lewry and I were the two not playing, so when the game started we sat on the balcony, soaking up the sun and having a bit of a laugh about this and that. I remember Jason remarking on how things had worked out quite well for me in the end: I'd have a few games before the end of the season to show just what I could do. As for Mooresy, it seemed that as the day went on, he was getting more and more – the only word I can think of is aloof. Maybe distant is more like it. I couldn't figure it out. There was something not right. About five o'clock I asked him if there was any chance of practising with him before we set off to Colwyn Bay tomorrow. He didn't answer me, just said would I follow him to the dressing room. Once again I felt that familiar feeling, that uneasiness, queasiness even. Yes, I reckoned I knew this scenario okay. 'Sorry mate, but you're not selected.' Or maybe I was wrong. Maybe it was, 'Look Waz, you need to make the most of these opportunities because here we are in August and you've only got four games left to earn that contract.'

I was wrong. Very wrong. The scenario was a new one for me, and it came right out of the blue. Pete sat me down, looked at the

CHAPTER 19 : 12TH MAN WITH A TWIST

ground and said, 'Waz, I don't know how to tell you this, it's the most difficult thing for me to say but that meeting we had on Friday....'

'Yes?'

'It was decided that the club were going to release you.'

CHAPTER 20

Opening bat for hire — cheap

I WAS grasping around for something to say, but nothing came. From outside I heard the 'tonk' of a big hit, and a few 'oohs' as the crowd broke into polite applause. It was like being outside a house where a party was going on, knowing you weren't going to be invited in. Next thing I heard Mooresy saying that, yes, he knew I hadn't had the opportunities like some of the others had, and he knew how hard I'd worked this year and yes, I'd done everything the club had asked of me, but unfortunately the decision had been made, and...

I was thinking fast. Grizz had got his way, hadn't he? He'd established Toby in the side and kept me out. Looking at the figures, if you told someone that an opening bat had stayed in the side for two seasons and this year he hadn't even averaged 20 they'd tell you it was simply laughable. No one could be worth a place on those stats. You wouldn't even be doing the guy a favour by

CHAPTER 20 : OPENING BAT FOR HIRE – CHEAP

picking him. Of course, this late in the season, if they had slotted me in and I'd done well it would throw a spanner in the works. The last thing they wanted now was to have to give me a new contract, and if I bounced back they'd more or less be obliged to. Now I saw it, plain as day.

As Mooresy sat there, twiddling with his sun visor and staring at the floor, I could see his unease. He had genuinely wanted me to do well, and he knew how hard I'd worked. What I couldn't understand was the way this whole thing had been handled. Here I was being sacked, out of a job for the first time in my life, and they'd obviously made their minds up on Friday, but they'd still had me in for 12th-man duties on a Sunday, and even then the decision had only come out when I asked Mooresy about a practice session for a match he knew I hadn't a cat in hell's chance of playing in. I found myself wondering what would have happened if I'd carried on chatting with the lads there. It had all been horribly mismanaged, and it raised all kinds of questions. Had it just been left to Mooresy to carry the can? And why not at least ask me to stay on for the final few weeks? They could have let me play, knowing I would go all out to impress other teams. This way they were rocking the boat, causing disharmony in the side. You had to ask the question, how professional were they being? Were they focussed on the promotion push, or were internal politics getting in the way?

Mooresy had run out of things to say, and I certainly couldn't think of anything. He asked me if I wanted to leave the ground now, even though the match was still in progress. Of course I did. I was gutted, stunned, disgusted. I went out into the glorious late summer sunshine and walked across to where Jason was sitting watching the game.

'What was that about?' he asked.

'It seems I'm not getting a new contract.'

'You what?'

'I'm out, mate. No new contract. Meet Wasim Khan, formerly of Sussex.'

'Oh shit, Waz. Have you got another county lined up?'

'No. Why would I? I never saw this coming.'

'Christ, that's awful, mate. But at least you've a few games to put yourself in the shop window.'

'No I haven't. He told me I can leave right now.'

'What, and leave us with one bloody opener in the entire squad?'

'Jason, mate, that ain't my problem any more.'

CHAPTER 20 : OPENING BAT FOR HIRE – CHEAP

'But the guys have all been assuming you'd get a run. We need someone who can do the opener thing.'

I was tempted to mention Toby's name, sorely tempted, but when it comes down to it I'm not really a sour grapes person. Anyway, they had an alternative – although what they did was, in my view, even worse than the way they sacked me. They handed the opening berth to Michael Yardy, who'd been batting at four and five for the seconds all season. Opening is a specialist position, and he was being thrown in at the deep end and asked to perform miracles. It wasn't fair to me, it wasn't fair to the club, and it certainly wasn't fair to Michael.

I left Eastbourne and drove home, still in my tracksuit, to regroup. It wasn't long before the phone started ringing as news spread among the guys. On the way I'd been having a little bet with myself as to who would call and who wouldn't. I wasn't far wrong. One of the first was Robin Martin-Jenkins, then Monty, and by the middle of the next day I reckoned I'd won the other part of my bet: Chris Adams never called. Neither did Dave Gilbert.

On the Monday morning I went to see Mooresy. I had no problem with the guy. He was doing his job, and at least he'd found the courage to tell me face to face that I was out. I never heard anything from Dave Gilbert, and I think that says a lot about the sort of man he was. Mooresy had said he would put in a word for me around the circuit, and I appreciated that. While we were talking Grizz came in. He said if I needed his help in any way he'd do what he could, but I don't think I really would have wanted to ask him. He'd stood in my way for two years, and I only had a bad taste in my mouth when I saw him. I told him I'd be okay. Later on, yes, we'd bump into each other as you do around the little world that is county cricket, and things would be okay between us. I actually like the guy now. I don't bear grudges, and I don't think he does. It's water under the bridge. But right then, hard on the heels of my humiliation, I wouldn't have asked him to stretch out his hand if I'd been drowning.

I left Mooresy's office for the last time with a mixture of sadness and relief. Sadness because I liked Hove and could have been very happy there, relief because now I could concentrate on planning my next move. At least there would be no more 'what ifs' that season. After I'd collected my things from the dressing-room and bunged them into a bin-bag, I walked around to where my car was parked. It was another gorgeous day and the ground-staff were

CHAPTER 20 : OPENING BAT FOR HIRE – CHEAP

setting out the deck chairs along one side in preparation for the next game. Across the road the lunchtime drinkers were gathered outside the Cricketers pub, laughing and joking. I took a last look at the wrought iron gates I'd come through as a new recruit from the champion county and slipped away, unobserved. I took my gear back to the flat and sat having a quiet drink of tea. I think that's when it hit me that I really wasn't a Sussex player any more; unless an offer came along pretty soon I was no longer a professional cricketer. That really put the fear of God into me.

I wrote a letter to Michael Yardy, wishing him the best of luck for his debut against Glamorgan. I really felt for the guy. As it turned out, he struggled and so did the team. Glamorgan piled up a total of over 600 in their first innings and won the game comfortably. As I set about working my contacts around the counties, Sussex wilted badly in their quest for promotion. It was strangely consoling to watch it all unfold on Teletext.

My problem now was that I'd hardly had any first-team action in the last two years, so it wasn't going to be easy to persuade people to get excited about my sudden availability. People have short memories. Players are always disappearing off the radar, and you forget about them. It's only rarely that you find yourself wondering 'whatever happened to so-and-so?' Maybe that was what was to be my fate: what happened to that Wasim guy? Mooresy had made a couple of enquiries, he told me, but nothing came of them. As the first of the autumn gales lashed the Brighton seafront I braced myself for a long hard winter.

Not only had the weather changed, but the cricketing climate was suddenly a lot less favourable. Clubs were feeling another financial squeeze and preferred to go with younger, and therefore cheaper players, single guys still consumed with a passion to play, guys who'd do it for peanuts. That's not to say that I wasn't desperate to play. I was, but unlike the younger guys I had a mortgage to pay. I was past the stage of sharing a flat with a bunch of young lads and taking my washing home to Mum once a month.

For my mental health I needed to keep active. I'd seen a Diploma course in Personal Training and Sports Therapy, right on my doorstep in Brighton. It ran from November to February, at the David Lloyd sports centre. Included in the programme was a Pitman computer course. What did I have in mind? I hadn't any real idea, but there was no way I was going to let my mind go to pot,

CHAPTER 20 : OPENING BAT FOR HIRE – CHEAP

any more than I'd neglect my body. Whatever happened, I had to keep busy.

Around this time I bumped into Tim Munton at the Professional Cricketers' Association annual dinner. I'd always liked Tim, who was now vice-captain at Derbyshire. He told me I was one of three players the club were looking at as possible recruits. They had another former colleague of mine from Warwickshire on the staff, Graeme Welch, so it all augured well. Tim and Graeme knew me, knew I was okay in the dressing-room. That's a big part of choosing a new member of a squad: it's all very well looking at a player's form or stats, but you need to know whether he's the kind of person who'll blend in with the team, be a positive influence on the squad at practice and in the field. Maybe that was the problem between me and Grizz: we simply weren't destined to get on.

While Tim promised to do his best for me – and I'm sure he did – he was constantly thwarted by administrative hold-ups, postponed meetings and airy promises. The course, meanwhile, was taking up five full days, Monday to Friday. I was with a good bunch of people and it was channelling my energies into something constructive. To this day I retain my masseur's qualification. I was taking it all in, but every spare moment I was out in the corridors checking my phone, hoping against hope that Tim would have something for me. The course was costing me money, and as autumn turned into winter it became more and more urgent for me to secure something for next season.

A couple of weeks before Christmas I did get a call to say that, yes, there was to be a meeting on the 18th and my fate should be decided then. Tim was confident; I was desperate. Oddly, as the winter wore on, I realised that although money was important, it wasn't actually my main consideration. The fact was, I wanted to play cricket – at any price. Maybe I was foolish, but I told Tim I would take whatever Derbyshire were willing to offer. It was mostly a desire to play the game, but also a fear – a dread of what it would feel like *not* to play. Cricket was all I'd known, all I'd ever wanted to know. I'd never given much thought to my playing career coming to an end. In an abstract sort of way I'd always known it would do, but it had always seemed a long, long way off – unimaginably remote. Then I started to wonder. I believed in Fate, in Allah's will; maybe this was His doing. But how could I know? And should I fight it or accept it? Was there a plan for me that had yet to be revealed? You can never know these things, of course, but you can

CHAPTER 20 : OPENING BAT FOR HIRE – CHEAP

decide that you're prepared to accept whatever happens. I wasn't ready for that yet. The thought that the plan might involve me turning my back on a playing career was too painful to contemplate.

I counted down the days before the Derbyshire meeting, hoping that it would finally bring an end to the uncertainty. The 18th came, and still no news. Was that a good sign or a bad one? Should I contact Tim or wait? I had reading to do for my course, but no way could I concentrate. That evening I sat in my flat, reading the same paragraph over and over, waiting and hoping for the call that never came. It was only a couple of days before Christmas when I gave in. I picked up the phone and dialled Tim's number.

'Oh sorry, Waz, didn't I tell you? They postponed the meeting.'

'Till when?'

'Well, it'll be after Christmas now.'

I knew what that meant. As far as most people in this country are concerned 'after Christmas' means sometime in mid-January. I'd have forked out another mortgage payment by then, and I wouldn't be surprised if I was still reading the same bloody paragraph of *The Skeletal Atlas*.

Weary and confused, I decided to go home for a few days break. To my parents' generation Christmas meant nothing, but we youngsters had all grown up with an air of festivity and liked to join in to some degree – even if it was no more than a chance to meet up with old friends and sit around watching repeats of *Only Fools and Horses*. Of course everyone wanted to know what was happening with Derbyshire. I wondered whether I ought to contact Raja. He had been responsible for helping one or two of the boys at Warwickshire obtain contracts at other counties. Yes, everyone was saying, he's the guy to see. He'd help me out. He had the contacts. He could probably get me a sponsor. If it was right that certain counties wanted me, but were struggling to find the money to pay me, he'd look around for some wealthy businessman in the area who would, effectively, pay my wages. There were plenty of Asian guys doing well in business, and most of them were cricketmad. They'd jump at the chance to get involved, surely.

Over the past few years a number of Asian players have, to my knowledge, had substantial support in this way: Kadir and Kabir Ali at Worcestershire, for a start, and the brothers Rawait and Zubair Khan at Derbyshire. For the counties it's a no-lose situation: they get talented young cricketers for virtually no outlay. If the guys come good, fine; if they don't make the grade,

CHAPTER 20 : OPENING BAT FOR HIRE – CHEAP

well, cheerio lads, and it's been nice having you on board. There's no contract to pay off. Wonderful. And why not? Cricket is still one of the poorest sports. England needs its counties to produce the next crop of Test players, but three or four-day Championship games will never attract the crowds, so there's very little income at county level. The game has to be inventive in the way it finds financial support. Maybe individual sponsorship is one way forward. I wasn't going to turn my nose up at it in 2001, no way.

I called Raja and went over to see him. We talked about who might be in a position to help me and we both came up with the same name. This was a marketing man. I was a bit dubious, because the same guy had promised to sort me out with a car some years ago, and the car had never quite materialised. But this was different, I told myself, and Raja agreed. When I went to meet the guy he was full of ideas. Yes, he had plenty of contacts. Yes, they were all cricket nuts. Yes, relax. Leave it with him and he'd sort it out.

When I told Tim what was going on he was chuffed to bits. This would surely clear the last obstacle. Raja, on the other hand, had been thinking. No need to make things too easy for Derbyshire. Why not contact

Gloucestershire as well? I got hold of Tony Wright, their second-team coach, and we arranged a meeting in Bristol: me and Raja, Tony, plus first-team coach John Bracewell. The first thing Tony wanted to know, not surprisingly, was what had gone wrong between Chris Adams and me. I was perfectly honest about the whole thing: the apparent clash of personalities, the broken promise, the row, the year and more of non-communication. Tony and John seemed satisfied, and Raj and I left there feeling we'd had a successful meeting.

While Tim was keen for me to join him at Derbyshire, he knew how desperate I was, so he agreed to help me any way he could. He'd been in touch with Gus Fraser at Middlesex and told him about my situation – namely, that I was a free agent and would have a sponsor for the coming season. In the end, however, the Middlesex deal came to nothing, and the Gloucestershire interest fizzled out at the same time. Tony Wright did call, but only to say that they'd decided it would be better to invest in a couple of younger players. I could understand that. I'd been effectively out of action for two years and was coming up to 30. Was that an enticing prospect?

However, I remained positive about Derbyshire. With Tim fighting my corner,

CHAPTER 20 : OPENING BAT FOR HIRE – CHEAP

surely I had every chance. Meanwhile, the calendar flipped relentlessly forward. My course was coming to an end and it would soon be time to think about serious pre-season training. Eventually I had a call from Tim, but only to tell me there would be another meeting in a few days' time. What the hell was going on? It now seemed that they were having the proverbial meetings about meetings. Had they no sense of urgency?

All this time I was talking about my situation to anyone who would listen, partly to get it off my chest, partly to see if anyone, anywhere, had an idea as to how I could break the vicious circle I was caught in: no interest because I'd been off the radar so long; no chance of getting back on the radar until somebody showed some interest. Among the people I spoke to was my old batting partner Andy Moles. After a successful benefit year at Warwickshire he'd landed on his feet: a five-year contract as coach to the Orange Free State. He was now living out there with his family in Bloemfontain and immediately wanted to know if I fancied going out and practising with the state side. Did I? I was online looking for a flight before I'd even looked the place up on the map.

I managed to get a cheap ticket for the first day of February, which meant I had just a couple of weeks to get something nailed down for the coming season. I chased up Tim, but the meeting at Derby was still 'on the agenda'. I chased up my contact to find out how the sponsorship was coming along. Listen I said, I'm off to South Africa in a fortnight. Sure, he said; you concentrate on your cricket and I'll see to things this end. We'll stay in touch by email. There seemed to be nothing else I could do, but then, just before I left, I got the news I wanted, a call from Colin Wells, the coach at Derby. Yes, they wanted me. He was even coming down to Brighton to take me out to lunch. This was a fantastic break. Now I could look forward to my trip to Bloemfontain as preparation for another season in English county cricket. Perfect.

When I met up with Colin, however, I was a little unnerved. He told me he saw me fitting perfectly into their one-day squad. I wondered whether he'd done any research on me. I'd spent my entire career playing three and four-day cricket, and had generally been overlooked for the one-dayers. I'd never even developed a proper strategy for that style of cricket. As to the four-dayers, he now told me I wouldn't be starting off in the side. He wanted to see how things turned out. This put me in a real dilemma: should I question it now and risk

CHAPTER 20 : OPENING BAT FOR HIRE – CHEAP

my immediate future, or keep quiet and risk it all falling apart later on? Before I had a chance to make my mind up on that Colin was asking me about my sponsorship deal. I filled him in and told him there were no worries there.

Despite what I told Colin, I was now starting to get seriously concerned about the guy who was supposed to be coming up with a sponsor. He was now in effect acting as my agent. Could I trust him? There was a huge amount hanging on it, and he seemed to have a lot of fingers in a lot of pies. All I could do, however, was wait – and enjoy my time in South Africa. Back in Hove I shoved my most precious possessions in a secure cupboard, got an agent to let the flat out, and set off for the airport.

I stayed with Moler, tried to unwind and enjoy family life. If we went out in the evenings it was generally to a restaurant. Bloemfontain was not really a party town in the way that Sydney is. Alan had arranged for me to do a bit of coaching with youngsters at the Orange Free State ground where I met up with Allan Donald, who was now playing for his home state. But really, this was no more than an interlude in a troubled time. The break was welcome, and I managed to play a couple of games for a local side, Aztex, but always on my mind was the need to set aside time to think about the future. All my life up until now I'd had this one driving passion, to get to the top as a cricketer. Now that the dream was fading, I was hoping at least to hang on in the game, somehow, somewhere. But as yet, nothing. Perhaps I was hoping for too much. How many people are lucky enough to earn a living doing something that stirs their very soul? Nevertheless, the one thing I did enjoy in Africa was the coaching – passing on the skills and knowledge that I'd picked up at the hands of old pros years ago, here and there imparting a little of the wisdom I felt I'd accrued along the way.

CHAPTER 21

Thanks for the memories

BACK home in Birmingham, with the season only weeks away now, I got a call from Raj. 'What's happening with this guy, Waz? Derby want to know. They're getting impatient.' It was 25 March and the deadline Derbyshire had set was a little over a week away. I called my contact. Yes yes, he said, the guy's still up for it, but I'm checking out a couple of other possibilities. The next thing I knew there was a letter on the doormat from Derby. This was a Monday morning and I had a week to produce a written statement from my sponsor confirming that he would pay my salary for the season. I called my contact in a panic. Look, I said, we've only got a few days to go. But the guy still didn't seem to understand.

Thursday came, and still no news. I called again. Yes, he had the sponsor ready to sign but he didn't really want to use that one and was negotiating with another. With hindsight, I should have read the signs far sooner. But I didn't. All I was thinking about was the possible end result: a continuation of the career I'd given everything for. Friday passed, and Saturday. This was insane. Sunday afternoon I called the guy once more. Under pressure, he cracked. As I sat there in my Mum's living-room he admitted, on the phone, that he had failed. He hadn't got a sponsor sorted out at all, and now he didn't know what to do. Before I knew it he was turning the collapse of my hopes into his own personal calamity. Next thing, I thought, he'd be asking me to have pity on him. I left him to his hand-wringing and got onto Raja. Help me, man, this guy's hung me out to dry.

We ended up, Raj and I, running around Birmingham like madmen that Sunday evening, driving from house to house desperately trying to find someone – anyone – who'd write the letter. Never mind the money, just write the letter. Please. In the end we got a mate called Max, a guy we knew in the mobile phone business. Raj and I more or less dictated the letter to him, and at nine o'clock next morning I hand-delivered it to the club. Job done.

Of course, the letter was just a stalling device. Max was no way going to sponsor me. He couldn't afford it. Now we had to get back to this so-called fixer and get him to find me another sponsor. I invited him to a pre-season friendly against Yorkshire and he was welcomed into the committee room.

CHAPTER 21 : THANKS FOR THE MEMORIES

He had recovered his composure by now, and of course everything was under control. It was just a matter of time. Everything would
be fine. I told him that BBC Midlands were coming to the ground on Monday to film the photo-call. Ah yes, he said, that would be an ideal time to unveil the sponsor. He'd call me over the weekend to iron out the details. I fell for it. I told the club they could look forward to finally meeting my benefactor on Monday and maybe put him in front of the TV cameras, do an interview with the new face of player recruitment. But it didn't happen. I never saw the guy again. If I had done I might have been tempted to give him a new face. At least, that's what I was telling people at the time.

So now I embarked on my Derbyshire career, as an amateur. Not officially: nobody knew my secret. As far as Tim and the guys were concerned I'd landed a sponsorship deal with some unnamed Asian businessman who always wanted to be cricketer himself but was too busy making piles of money. It was a plausible story.

The whole set-up at Derby was very different from what I'd experienced at Warwickshire, a Test county run on such professional lines, and even at Sussex, smaller, but with a hard-working staff who were trying to build something – and for a while succeeding. At Derby the Chief Exec was a young guy called John Smedley – outgoing, amiable and refreshingly lacking in airs and graces. But it did seem odd the way we all had a laugh and a joke with him as if he were just one of the boys. You don't want your upper management to be remote, but you do feel that they should maintain a certain distance. After all, they have the final say in hiring and firing players.

All things considered, I didn't have a good time at Derby. If I remember it for anything it's for the successive low points. The only laughs I recall were when I reflected on the irony of ending up there. In the past, whenever we'd played at Derby, all the Warwickshire lads had agreed that it was the worst place on the circuit: the weather was always cold and miserable and the ground lacked any charm or atmosphere. It was more like an out-ground than a county headquarters, with its little pavilion and the open side where punters drove up almost to the boundary rope and pulled out their deck-chairs and windbreaks. I did hear one or two old-timers say, 'At least you never had to play at Ashby-de-la-Zouch', but the Leicestershire venue was decommissioned as a county ground well before our time.

CHAPTER 21 : THANKS FOR THE MEMORIES

Still, they were a decent bunch of lads. And they still had one of my old antagonists, Dominic Cork, in the side. He was the captain, very much the big fish in the small pond, and seemed to run the playing side. He even tried to take charge of practice. I once saw him grab the whiteboard off Colin Wells, write up a batting order for the nets, and for fielding practice, before handing it back to a gobsmacked coach. He seemed to be a major influence off the field. But by and large, he had everyone's respect, so it wasn't a case of him trying to lord it over them as the big-time Charlie. It was all part of his natural exuberance.

Given my financial circumstances, I suppose I could have lived in Brum and travelled to and fro, but the last thing I wanted was to be driving two or three hours a day. Besides, back home there was still this pressure for me to settle down and raise a family. So I had an introduction to a scene I'd never really experienced before – apart from my first couple of trips Down Under. The club sorted me out a house in Littleover, sharing with my old teammate Graeme Welch and Chris Basano. Bassy had come to Derby from Australia, but his father was South African. However, he had just enough English blood on his mother's side to qualify as a non-overseas player. He kicked off his season in fantastic style, knocking up two hundreds on his debut against Gloucestershire.

There was one Asian lad at Derby, Rawait Khan, a class player who looked as though he had a real future ahead of him. He really had managed to get a sponsor for the season, so he wasn't costing the county anything either. As for me, I couldn't ignore the fact that things just weren't working out. Although I kept myself in tip-top condition and continued to work on my game I knew I was losing the edge. Cricket, more than most games, is played in the mind, and my mind wasn't really right after the barren years at Sussex. I'd become dispirited, my self-confidence had been eroded, and because of the lack of chances at four-day level, I was short of match practice. I simply wasn't as sharp as I wanted to be.

Going to Derby was a mistake. Colin Wells had me down as a one-day player, and I wasn't. Never had been, never would be. I'm sure I could've been, but throughout my career nobody had ever made a point of it. I muddled along as well as I could, playing wherever they wanted me, batting in the middle to lower order where you needed to get your eye in immediately and score runs fast. That simply wasn't my style, and I

CHAPTER 21 : THANKS FOR THE MEMORIES

generally failed. As for the four-day version, my entire season in the first XI had a grotesque symmetry to it: one match, one innings, one run.

Around the middle of the season I came clean with the captain about my situation. Graeme couldn't believe what I was telling him, that I was playing for nothing. I explained how I thought it had been worth a last gambler's throw of the dice: keep playing, get a bit of form, and maybe secure a contract the following year. But in the end my situation wore me down. I lost confidence, I lost form, I lost self-respect. When the boys were getting their cheques at the end of every month and wanting to go out on the town, I was wincing as I saw yet another clutch of monthly expenses haemorrhaging out of my bank account.

To be fair to the boys at Derby, they were great through all this. They did everything they could to make me feel welcome. However, I didn't find Colin Wells the most communicative of guys, and I still questioned his professionalism in bringing me into the Derby set-up as a one-day player. That was just plain daft, and it must have become obvious even to him in the end.

There comes a time when perseverance isn't enough. In fact, there comes a time when it's damaging to your self-esteem to keep on banging your head against a brick wall. I was mowing the grass – not at the ground, but at the house in Littleover. It's the kind of mindless task that allows you to reflect, and I had plenty to think back on. It was only six years ago that I was on the balcony having my photo taken with the NatWest Cup, part of an all-conquering Warwickshire team. Now I was stuck in the seconds at a second-rate county with a bunch of 20-year-olds, living in a rented place in a town I didn't like and pushing a mower back and forth because my housemates were off playing for the first team. As I tipped another pile of damp clippings into the compost-heap in a dank corner of the garden, I realised quite clearly what I had to do.

Next morning I drove to the ground and found Tim. I told him I had had enough. I was going to call it a day. Tim told me not to be hasty. There were five or six weeks of the season left, and who knew what would happen? But I was past the point where I truly hoped for a turnaround, and the fact that my financial resources were dwindling was starting to take precedence over the other considerations. If I wasn't going to play Championship cricket as a contracted pro, then it was time I looked for something else to do with my life. Above all I wanted to go with dignity, of my own volition, before someone

CHAPTER 21 : THANKS FOR THE MEMORIES

had to call me into a dressing-room, clear his throat and stare at the floor and tell me tactfully, Waz mate, the game's up.

As I drove back to Littleover, pondering the future, it occurred to me that I'd always known deep down that cricket was, essentially, an escape from reality. It's a cocooned world, and the more comfortable you are in it the more you just hope it'll carry on forever. For a cricketer the future is a cold, unknown place where there's no team to back you up, no gentle applause to caress your ego, no endless summer days on England's green and velvety pitches, and no sunny winters in the land of plenty. No, for a cricketer confronting the end of his career the future doesn't bear thinking about. I'd certainly managed to keep it off my personal agenda. Now I looked at my own situation through the magnifying glass. In August 2001 it wasn't good. I'd concentrated on cricket from an early age and neglected my education. What would I do now that the show was over?

The next day, as I carried up my things from the house in Littleover and stuffed them into the car, I wasn't ready to think about the long-term future. I wanted to be back in Small Heath, where I would be surrounded by people who loved me. I'd sort the rest out from the safety and security of home.

As I closed the front door and posted my key through the letterbox, I looked at my watch and saw the number, 12. It was 12 August, six years to the day since that glorious moment when I'd notched my maiden first-class hundred. Back then the dream had been unfolding stage by stage; it seemed unstoppable. As I stepped up through the sgrades I'd done well at every level. Was there any reason why it shouldn't continue? Next stop, surely, would be a call – up for the England team, and I'd be walking out at Lord's to face my father's nation, then...

I drove home with my car crammed full of clothes and kit, my alarm clock and toaster, breathing in the scents of the spices I'd collected as I tried to imitate my mother's curries rather than splash out on a restaurant meal. To the other drivers I passed on the road, seeing the dressing gown stuffed in the rear window next to the laundry basket full of bedding, I might have been a student going home after graduating. But I hadn't got the satisfaction of a degree in my back pocket. All I'd got was broken promises and unfulfilled hopes. The salt taste of disappointment was in my mouth, but at the same time I knew that after what I'd been through over the past three years the next few would surely be better. I would make them better.

CHAPTER 22

Back where I started

MY MUM, at least, was glad I was home. Of course she would have loved to see me hit the heights in my chosen career, but for her the consolation of my failure was that I would be around the place a little more. After three years she'd have a man in the house again. Actually, she had a male presence already, since my sister was living there with her husband. But to Mum, I was the man of the family, as agreed when Dad had died, and now I was back.

When people in the neighbourhood started asked me what I was doing, I had to get used to saying – as I was justified in saying – that I'd retired from cricket. I hadn't been sacked; I'd decided to finish it. People were staggered that I could retire so young. Really? You've retired? Yes, I answered. But surely that meant I was rich? If only they knew the truth.

One day when I'd been home a couple of weeks I went for a stroll around the neighbourhood. For the first week or two I'd been wary about going out too much. I knew that eventually I'd bump into the guy who'd let me down so badly over the phantom sponsor, and I knew I needed to avoid him while I was still hurting so much inside. But I was out now, and walking past Oldknow School. I stopped there to watch the young kids playing – football, of course, since it was now September. I thought about me and Amjad, and poor Parvaz, three future county cricketers, playing our epic Test Matches there; I thought of all the balls we'd pinched; I thought of Pete Bolland coming out to give us grief, and then on an impulse asking me to do that forward defensive for him. I thought too of the other guys I'd grown up with. Raja, assistant manager with the Pakistani team and teaching in Birmingham; my next-door neighbour Gary Smith, a semi-pro for Tamworth Town football club, later summoned by a fax to represent his Mum's country, St Kitts, in a World Cup qualifier against the Turks and Cacos Islands; Paul Kenna, a major local influence through his love for the community, the one white guy everyone knew and trusted; and then the guys like Amjad who hadn't quite made it but had wound up as a club pro with Berkeswell, was married at 20, now drove a taxi – and was happy; Akhlaq, who'd gone to work in the cargo bays at Birmingham airport and would end up a vice – president for Serviceair; Liaquat

CHAPTER 22 : BACK WHERE I STARTED

Ali, perhaps the brightest of us all, now a postman.

Suddenly a big smile had spread across my face. They'd been such good days, and I'd been one of a whole crop of kids who'd had the good fortune to be young when so much was possible. That grimy tarmac playground there, it had been our very own field of dreams. As I watched the kids scuffling for the ball in a corner I realised that I wasn't a failure. No, I had been a success. It wasn't as if I'd come from a public school, full of expectation and self-confidence, nurtured on velvety green pitches under spreading broad-leafed trees. I'd come from a grotty little inner-city Victorian school and had learned to play in the street, 20-a-side games. Thanks to one schoolmaster who showed an interest, and thanks to my passion for the game, I had emerged from what we used to call the ghetto and become . . . a professional cricketer. Forget the failures; look at the achievements: from Small Heath to Edgbaston, from Oldknow School to Warwickshire first XI and a Championship medal; from Somerville Road to Sydney. If the clock had stopped with that maiden hundred, or at the end of the wonderful 1995 season, I would have been a legend.

It was October when I made my mind up, and I'm sure that my little stroll by the old school was a big part of the decision I now made. Cricket had given me a way out of the narrow streets and back alleys of Small Heath to a wider world. It had taken me around the globe, it had taught me new skills, from eating with cutlery to conversing with people from all sorts of cultures and classes, to ways of living a healthy and fruitful life. It had made a man of me and given me, even in comparative failure, a self-belief and a strength. Cricket was what I knew, and cricket was what I had to offer. And I realised now what it could offer to the next generation of kids if we could catch them early enough. I would coach youngsters, show them the joys of the great game, and hopefully give them a new horizon beyond the place where they grew up.

How wonderful, then, that my first opportunity to teach a few skills came right there at my old school. And how fortuitous that, having spoken to Pete Slough, the new headmaster at Oldknow, now amalgamated with a neighbouring institution as Small Heath School, I spotted an opportunity to get involved at the school. The thought of getting in someone with my experience as a coach, organiser and role model – well, it was just what he was looking for. It had simply never occurred to him that such a paragon existed.

CHAPTER 22 : BACK WHERE I STARTED

A day or two later I got a formal approach from Pete. Then it was time to meet and discuss practicalities. When could I start? I didn't exactly have to check the diary. Every page was blank just now. Could I come in for a couple of hours, say two days a week? At £40 an hour? Now it was my turn to snap at an extended hand.

In the context of much that's happened to me over the past three or four years, you might say that these were small beginnings, but at the time it was as if I was in a big dark building full of menacing echoes, and a very large door was creaking slowly open. I didn't really know what lay on the other side of it, but I could see sunshine there, and blue sky, and I knew I wanted to be out in it. More importantly, I realised that whereas I was tempted to see myself as having failed, there were people out there – teachers, schoolkids, my neighbours – to whom my story so far had been a huge success.

I started out running after-school clubs, mostly for boys, just about all of them Asian – that was the ethnic make – up of the school and the neighbourhood – and mostly years 7 to 10, that is kids aged 12 to 15, about the age Amjad, Parvaz and I had been when Pete Bolland took us under his wing. I worked with Norman Hewison, the head of PE. Where my mates and I had made do with some pretty basic equipment before we got to Edgbaston, these kids had the advantage of block bookings at the leisure centre where there were plenty of bats, balls and pads. This is where I started to realise how much they had to learn. Most of them had grown up playing cricket, but without any structure at all. It had been the cricketing equivalent of a kickaround. I had more than one lad trying to tie his pads on back to front, and of course when I handed out the boxes there was an outburst of merriment. While some of them were keen to look the part and get all kitted up with protective wear, others thought it was a bit girlie. 'But sir, if you're hard, sir, you won't need all that gear will you sir?' They wouldn't be entirely cured of that until they met a genuine cricket ball. I decided it would be safer for all concerned if we started with the soft version.

As well as getting stuck into the various techniques of batting and bowling, I instructed them in how to warm up at the start of every session; I talked about diet and tried to hammer home the anti-junk food message – but of course if ever I was around at lunchtime I'd see most of them queuing up outside the chip shops and burger bars that have sprung up around all the schools these days. By and large, their

CHAPTER 22 : BACK WHERE I STARTED

level of fitness was atrocious. They had none of the nimbleness that we had as youngsters, when we were always on our toes ready to duck out of the way of a passing car, darting across the road to take a high catch, or running away from an irate mother whose windows had just been rattled by a lofted cover-drive.

In these and in other ways the whole process of trying to provide the kids with an education in how to look after their bodies was a learning curve for me. Here I was, barely 15 years older than them, shocked by their general lack of discipline, the problem they seemed to have with simply listening to what someone was saying to them, their lack of respect – not just for their elders, but for each other, and, worst of all, for their own bodies.

There was a lot to do. Once we got them playing various forms of cricket indoors with the soft ball we started thinking about other schools we could play against when the new season came around. We were all agreed that while this was valuable after – school activity, the kids weren't going to make significant progress until they started playing competitively. That would mean schools with decent grass fields; and it would probably mean posh schools, like King Edward's Grammar. But first I had to get the lads used to the hard ball. It wasn't easy, especially when it came to fielding. Like most beginners, they would stand with their legs wide apart, bend down and hope to snatch the ball up as it came through.

It reminded me of my own early days. As soon as the ball bounced or bobbled it'd be through them and away. The idea of getting a knee or an ankle in the way horrified them. 'But it'll hit me, sir.' 'I done that once sir. Look at this bruise.'

Towards the end of that first term I finally bumped into the guy who had led me such a dance over the sponsorship deal. It was, in the end, almost comical. I was preoccupied with what I was now doing, and he greeted me with a big smile as if the events of the previous summer had never happened. Hi, how are things, and so on. Everything was fine, I told him. Good, good, good. The last thing he said to me was, 'And in the end I came up with the perfect sponsor – but you know you never called me back!' I had to laugh. From my point of view he was pathetic. I had other fish to fry.

Slowly we made progress. And, miraculously, word started to spread. Before October was out I had started getting calls from other schools. They had heard what I was doing with the lads at Small Heath. Could I come to them too? This was getting

CHAPTER 22 : BACK WHERE I STARTED

serious. It was time to set myself up as a business. I squeezed a table into Mum's tiny spare bedroom, installed a phone with a fax machine, a lap-top and a second-hand printer, made an appointment to see my bank manager, and announced to the world that Khan Kricket was up and running. Then I sat down and wrote to every school I could find listed in the Birmingham area.

Not only was I asked to do more coaching sessions than I could possibly manage single-handed, I was overwhelmed with requests to speak to school assemblies as a sort of role-model. During my first year I did one a week of those through term-time. I followed more or less the same pattern for each. After the head teacher had introduced me as an almost iconic figure, something between a rock star and a sporting super-hero, I made it my business to show the kids that I was, in fact, just like them.

'Where do you think I live then?'
'Solihull?'
'No.'
'Moseley?'
'No, I live in Small Heath.'
'Small Heath?'
'Yes, I was born and bred there.'

They were always amazed at that. Small Heath was where the dead-beats hung out, surely?

'Not when I was a kid.'

Then I'd talk about school and admit that, yes, I'd been a bit of a dosser. I'd tell them that I was the joker in the classroom, and ask them who was their class comedian. I'd talk about the swots, the geeks I was at school with, and isn't it strange how they're the guys now who have got on and live in the nice houses and drive the fancy cars – better ones than I can afford.

But you're doing okay, they said. Only because I was lucky, I told them. I was a chance discovery in the playground. It might never have happened. And after that – this is where I tried to put my serious face on – it was all down to work and a burning desire. I'd been 'brim full of passion'. It wasn't luck, nor favours, but hard graft; dedication; getting up at six in the morning, rain or shine, and running – even if you had had a late night. And eating the right things.

These sessions were terrific. I'd try to open it up for questions and answers, and immediately we'd start to hear the thing we all fall back on when things are going badly. It's not my fault; it's not fair; they're all against me because I'm short or spotty or different, or a Paki. Which led us to racism. Yes, I said, in the real world there is racism, but you have to use things like that to drive

CHAPTER 22 : BACK WHERE I STARTED

you forward. Do your best; try your hardest; decide you'll be a success despite it.

One thing soon led to another. From the original idea of cricket coaching another development emerged as I was asked to come up with programmes for interactive workshops for groups of maybe 15 to 20 disruptive kids. This was a challenge. From being a cricketing technician I had now to be a father figure and social worker, a mentor. It was, above all, emotionally tiring. The only real respite was when they started asking me questions about myself. They were intensely curious. Tell us about Australia, Wasim. Yeah, and playing at Edgbaston. And what about that Allan Donald? I bet he was bloody quick. Was he a racist, like all of them South Africans? By and large, I loved it when they asked me about my playing days. It was my chance to feel good about me, another chance to be a star. There I was supposedly helping these kids and without knowing it they were feeding my need, comforting me as I excavated my way out of the rubble of my collapsed dream.

CHAPTER 23

The ghetto boy and the Governor

THE actual coaching was now way beyond what I could handle on my own, so I started tapping up my old mates. Graeme Welch, Belly, the Warwickshire all-rounder Mohamed Sheikh – they all came to work for me in those early days. And as that side of things developed I realised I might as well spread the word as far up the cricketing tree as I could. I knew that Tim Munton and Gladstone Small now worked for the Professional Cricketers' Association, so I invited them to come up and watch one of the competitive events we'd managed to put on, a 30-school affair at Birmingham's National Indoor Arena. It was Kwik cricket, which the primary kids loved: there's so much less hanging about than in the conventional forms.

Gladstone was particularly impressed, and suggested I write an article for the PCA magazine. It would spread the word further, generate debate and raise my profile. Probably as a result of this exposure, the

CHAPTER 23 : THE GHETTO BOY AND THE GOVERNOR

PCA now approached me. They were setting up a major project in association with the Prince's Trust. Would I come aboard on a consultancy basis? The idea was to attach hard-to-reach youngsters to their counties by using professional players as mentors and coaches, with the physios providing sessions on health and fitness, motivation and social skills. My role would be to co-ordinate the efforts of the 18 counties, to liase with the clubs and set up programmes for these youngsters, taken largely from the ranks of the under-privileged. That meant kids who had spent much of their childhood in care and were coming out into the community. It meant educational under-achievers. It even meant kids who'd been detained for criminal activity.

This was a terrific break for me, although of course it took me more and more away from my own coaching school in Birmingham. I found the work of liasing with clubs and counties easy – or should I say it came naturally to me. There was too much of it for me to call it easy. I was now already drawing on the things I'd learned as a watchful, wary youngster from 'the ghetto'. How do other people relate to each other? How do they communicate? How do they rub along? In wanting to belong, I'd taught myself how to get by in most social situations, even to the extent of mimicking the white people I'd mixed with, learning their language so to speak. I now found myself equally at ease with county executives, local authority administrators, social workers and their often awkward charges.

At the same time my coaching set-up was thriving. I had a great team of guys working for me, all hand-picked. There was Rawait Khan, Mohamed Sheikh, Michael Bell, my old pal Amjad, and Parvaz's brother Manir Mirza. I really was in business now. But like any businessman, I found I never had any cash, and even less time. I seemed to be working 24 hours a day, seven days a week, and was extremely grateful for the £1,500 a month I was now receiving from the PCA.

I realised I needed to protect the business I had built up. Well, I say I realised it: I actually had to be told firmly by friends that this was the next step. My trouble was that I trusted people, and in business, you simply can't afford to do that. The last thing I needed was for some sharp operator to spot what I was doing, set himself up in competition and start waving the chequebook at my coaches. A friend of mine who worked for a big law firm in London drew up the necessary legal documents to protect the business. She advised me, and drafted contracts for my coaches to sign.

CHAPTER 23 : THE GHETTO BOY AND THE GOVERNOR

Still the thing continued to grow as new opportunities presented themselves. Out of the blue came a call from Newham in East London. The head of sport at a sixth – form college there wanted a series of workshops. Fifteen Sundays, starting as soon as possible. Early on in a new business you're too insecure ever to say no. Each chance could be the last. So every Sunday for four months I set off from home at six o'clock on a Sunday morning, picked up three or four of the guys and headed down the Ml, worked till lunchtime, then fought my way through the M25 traffic and home.

The credibility of Khan Kricket was now growing as we worked with 25 inner-city schools in Birmingham. Recruiting current and retired players as role models worked wonders, and we'd clearly tapped into a need for cricket not just as another game but as a way of improving the kids' self-esteem. Coaching in the nets was interspersed with counselling sessions as we tried to find ways to solve the kids' behavioural problems through sporting activity. But as the amount of work grew and I became more and more involved with the PCA there was a conflict brewing. I couldn't give myself fully to both. I tried, but I simply couldn't fulfil all my duties.

It all came to a head early in 2004 when the PCA offered me a full-time permanent position as their Community Development Manager. What that meant was doing the same as I'd been doing the last couple of years, but on a wider scale. Of course, I grabbed the opportunity with both hands, but at the same time I knew I had to make a decision about the coaching school. Should I let someone else take it over? I took advice, and reluctantly came to the conclusion that I should close it down. It was no good having a thing like that with my name on it run by people who, no matter how well motivated they were, would require some sort of supervision. I wouldn't be letting the schools down: they had got hold of the idea by now, and knew that it worked. They would find other people who could offer the services I'd provided. Warwickshire CCC themselves were by now committed to working in the community, linking up with the schemes I had been involved with. The only regret I have about the changes that had to take place is that now they tend to use county board coaches rather than current and former players. These guys do a great job, but the kids get such a buzz out of being taught by guys they've heard of, or maybe seen on TV.

Down in London with the PCA I looked at ways in which cricket could offer more innovative programmes. I set up a scheme

CHAPTER 23 : THE GHETTO BOY AND THE GOVERNOR

to use sport as a way of integrating the recent influx of refugees from the Balkan states and elsewhere into the mainstream of British society. It was easy for me to put my heart into that as I thought back to the way Amjad, Parvaz and I had mixed with the English, Irish and West Indians back in Somerville Road, and later how we'd warily gone along with the white guys after an under-19s game, and hovered fearfully outside the restaurants and pubs as they went inside before finally plucking up the courage to follow them. We had been raised to think of pubs as places where only one thing took place: drinking, which to us as Muslims was taboo. We never realised until we went inside that you could enjoy a pleasant meal, a soft drink and a game of pool or darts. Our horizons had been further broadened by playing with older guys from all walks of life in club cricket – and we'd all developed a taste for scampi and chips.

So it was clear to me that there were a lot of basic life skills which these migrants could learn from the experience of playing a very English game with a bunch of other kids from varied backgrounds. We drafted in guys like Carl Crowe, the former Leicestershire off-spinner, and Martin Speight, the ex-Sussex and Durham wicketkeeper. We brought in English kids to mix things up a bit and give the refugees a chance to learn the language and culture the way I learned it on the street, simply by playing and hanging out together, becoming mates. We found ourselves offering sessions on English life and culture – and I, a child of Kashmiri immigrants, found myself telling a new wave of incomers 'this is how we do things in this country'. Recognising that cricket is still a minority interest, we tried to expand into a more multi – sport approach. I approached Roger Reade at the Professional Footballers' Association and started setting up sessions with such football clubs as Leicester City. We even roped in the Basketball Association.

This was an exhilarating time for me. It seemed that there was enough goodwill out there to make anything possible. Knowing how important role models are, I set up the Team England Ambassadors Programme, recruiting six current England cricketers to representative roles in their own regions, their task being to raise the profile of our programmes by putting themselves in the limelight and letting local kids meet their heroes.

During the summer of 2005 the PCA seconded me for two days a week to manage some pilot programmes for a huge new initiative. *Chance to shine* is a campaign for the education and well-being of young people

CHAPTER 23 : THE GHETTO BOY AND THE GOVERNOR

run by the Cricket Foundation, a charitable arm of the England and Wales Cricket Board. It was launched with the aim of raising £50 million, one half from private donations and commercial organisations, the other half from matched Government funding. Here was a fantastic opportunity to strengthen my ties with the grassroots of the game and more importantly to help develop the life skills of young people. The budget for this scheme is as impressive as its scope is broad. In 10 years we aim to have 800 clubs and 6,700 schools, primary and secondary, involved in coaching programmes and competitive fixtures. As well as providing structured competition for the youngsters, we aim to extend the benefits through facility provision within state schools. By developing the next generation of teachers we will secure our legacy within the nation's school system and re-establish the great game – and its values – as the summer sport in this country. More than that, by planting the seeds of interest, involvement and technique, we hope to nurture a new generation of cricketers who will benefit enormously from the education afforded by structured competitive sport. Our hope is that these youngsters will in time pass on their love of the game, and knowledge of it, to the next generation, their own children.

Some of my friends wanted to know why the PCA would happily second me to work for a different outfit, the Cricket Foundation. They'd only had me a year, if that. The answer is that the PCA is always encouraging its members, and staff, to move on to bigger and better things. It is committed to individual development of past, present and future cricketers. Through increased investment in the areas of education, the PCA is arming players with tools and skills that will enable them to leave the cocoon of professional cricket better prepared for success in the real world.

When I was invited to apply for the full-time job of Director of Operations with the Cricket Foundation, I found myself making tracks not for Lord's but for Threadneedle Street. Chairing the interview panel was no less a person than the Governor of the Bank of England, Mervyn King. The President of the campaign is passionate about the game, and dedicated to the education and well-being of the young. He is convinced that his experiences as a school cricketer developed within him many of the qualities that have stood him in good stead throughout his long and successful career. He is not just a figurehead, but is active in the campaign on a daily basis.

CHAPTER 23 : THE GHETTO BOY AND THE GOVERNOR

When I went for the interview, I couldn't help thinking about what an old friend in Small Heath had said to me a couple of days earlier. It was a case, he said, of 'Ghetto boy meets Governor'. If I'd thought about it too hard I could have been intimidated, but once I discovered that I was being interviewed by a life-long Villa fan, I relaxed and gave him a bit of grief about the Blues' resurgence under Steve Bruce!

I was delighted to be given the job, and at the prospect of making things happen in what was now being hailed as the biggest ever grass-roots initiative in UK sport. What appealed to me was the emphasis on education and the development of life skills such as leadership, discipline and the acceptance of individual responsibility.

I had been interviewed by, among others, Mervyn King. But he is just one of the people fronting the set-up. Also on board are five vice-presidents, people like Sir Tim Rice, who has handed over a million pounds of his own money to the scheme. There is also Mark Nicholas, the Channel 4 presenter and former Hampshire captain, Lord Siraj Paul, the Labour peer and former steel magnate, Sir Bill Morris, the former trade union leader, and Lord Ian McLaurin, once the chief exec at Tesco, and more recently Chairman of the ECB. Having a team of this calibre has enabled the Cricket Foundation to maintain a high profile as well as grab the attention of an awful lot of other people of status who have helped with the funding drives.

The fact is that cricket has struggled for many years in the face of competition from so many other sports, especially football. Yet there is in this country a huge body of goodwill towards the game, never more evident than when Michael Vaughan's team prised the Ashes from the Australians' grasp in such dramatic fashion in the summer of 2005. As much as everyone wanted it to happen, even willed it to happen, public and pundits alike were realistic enough, or so they thought, to see it as an impossible dream, especially after the summer started with defeat in the Lord's Test. What happened at Edgbaston and afterwards created a tidal wave of euphoria and reminded a new generation of the amazing drama that the game of cricket is capable of brewing up – and of the remarkably good spirit in which an intensely competitive game can be played.

Launching *Chance to shine* prior to that Ashes series turned out to be a stroke of sheer genius (well, that's what we like to claim!). We could never have dreamed of the impact England's triumph would have on the

CHAPTER 23 : THE GHETTO BOY AND THE GOVERNOR

whole nation. From our point of view, waiting on the launch-pad, it was like having the tank filled with rocket propellant. Money flowed in from private donors and well-wishers, the press were suddenly seriously interested in not just the top end but also the grass roots of the great game, and schools and clubs were lining up to get involved. In the wake of that great summer we were able to recruit Matthew Hoggard to the cause. Originally he was asked if we could use his image on the leaflets. As soon as he became more aware of the objectives of our initiative he asked if he could stay, and he is now an important figurehead for us.

Suddenly cricket is sexy, and what we are doing has captured people's imagination. The Government has thrown its weight behind us, matching our funding drive pound for pound; the Barmy Army supports us, as do the PCA, ECB and the Lord's Taverners, who have committed a million pounds to the cause. Commercial sponsors and companies are getting involved and we are working hard to spread the message of a worthwhile cause.

My role has expanded beyond all my own expectations. To tell the truth, I had none when I started. It was a voyage into the unknown. Now my time is divided between Edgbaston and Lord's; I have responsibility for three regional managers, and through them close contact with everyone from cricketing administration to the Government.

*****

It may sound like a cliche to say that I've come a long way, but that's the simple truth. In fact, I think I've come further than many people close to me realise. In my opinion you measure a person's success not just by looking at where they end up in life, but by taking into account where they started from. When I reflect on the distance I have travelled I see a road that stretches back not just to Small Heath, but all the way to Kashmir and the decision my parents made to seek their own fortunes in England 40 years ago. That's where my story really began. My parents probably gave me the biggest break I ever had by making that journey.

I think back to something I found in one of the self-help books I read when I had time on my hands in various dressing-roms around the county cricket circuit. It was a quotation from Aldous Huxley, who said, 'Experience is not what happens to a man; it is what a man does with what happens to him.' I had the good fortune to live my dream for a season or two before things

CHAPTER 23 : THE GHETTO BOY AND THE GOVERNOR

went wrong. But now, strengthened by the various experiences of failure and success, nourished by the love of my beautiful wife Salma and the rest of my family, I find myself in a position to help a new generation benefit in so many ways from the great game of cricket. It couldn't really have worked out much better.

Chance to shine
BRINGING CRICKET TO STATE SCHOOLS

Chance to shine

The Cricket Foundation's Chance to shine is the biggest and most ambitious grass roots sports initiative ever launched. The aim is to regenerate competitive cricket in a third of state schools, and to reach over two million boys and girls. Launched in May 2005, the Appeal aims to raise £25 million over five years. This figure will be matched pound for pound by the government – so doubling the value of all donations. The money raised will provide more and better opportunities for boys and girls from all communities of our society, to be taught cricket and encouraged to play it regularly in competition at school.

The Appeal is led by its President, Mervyn King, Governor of the Bank of England. The five supporting Vice-Presidents are: Lord

(Ian) MacLaurin, Sir Bill Morris, Mark Nicholas, Lord (Swraj) Paul and Sir Tim Rice. Like all involved in the campaign the President and Vice-Presidents are driven by a concern first and foremost for the education and well-being of young people.

The Cricket Foundation is licensed by the ECB to assume direct responsibility for implementing, managing and monitoring Chance to shine programmes. Wasim Khan as Operations Director (OD) and a team of regional managers will strategically develop, monitor and manage the delivery of the programmes.

www.chancetoshine.org

www.ingramcontent.com/pod-product-compliance
Lightning Source LLC
Chambersburg PA
CBHW072003150426
43194CB00008B/986